LEARN TO MOVE, MOVING UP!

SENSORIMOTOR ELEMENTARY-SCHOOL ACTIVITY THEMES

LEARN TO MOVE, MOVING UP!

SENSORIMOTOR ELEMENTARY-SCHOOL ACTIVITY THEMES

Jenny Clark Brack, OTR/L, BCP AOTA Board Certification in Pediatrics

Photos by C. Scott Campbell
Cartoons by Gerard Arantowicz

APC

Autism Asperger Publishing Co.
P.O. Box 23173
Shawnee Mission, KS 66283-0173
www.asperger.net

© 2009 by Autism Asperger Publishing Company
P.O. Box 23173
Shawnee Mission, KS 66283-0173
www.asperger.net

All rights reserved. With the exception of pages 156-159, no part of the material protected by this copyright notice may be reproduced or used in any form or by any means, electronic or mechanical, including photocopying, recording, or by any information storage and retrieval system, without the prior written permission of the copyright owner.

Publisher's Cataloging-in-Publication

Brack, Jenny Clark, 1965-
  Learn to move, moving up! : sensorimotor elementary-school activity themes / Jenny Clark Brack ; photos and cartoons by Scott Campbell and Gerard Arantowicz. -- Shawnee Mission, KS : Autism Asperger Pub. Co., c2009.

   p. ; cm.
   ISBN: 978-1-934575-38-3
   LCCN: 2008941923

   Summary: A sequel for older students to the author's earlier book, "Learn to move, move to learn: sensorimotor early childhood activity themes". Presents a series of themed activities designed to improve children's sensory issues, making them ready to learn. Suggested curriculum ideas help ensure sensory issues are implemented throughout the curriculum.
   Includes bibliographical references.

   1. Autistic children--Education (Elementary) 2. Asperger's syndrome--Patients--Education (Elementary) 3. Sensory integration dysfunction in children. 4. Play therapy. 5. Early childhood education--Activity programs. I. Campbell, Scott (Charles Scott), 1958- II. Arantowicz, Gerard. III. Title.

LC4717.5 .B735 2009   2008941923
371.94--dc22   0812

This book is designed in DingleHopper and Helvetica Neue

Cover and Other Illustrations: Gerard Arantowicz

Printed in the United States of America

ACKNOWLEDGMENTS

I am deeply grateful for all the "curriculum suggestions" written by Chris Giebler, second-grade general education teacher at Scranton Elementary School, Scranton, Kansas. His educational perspective is invaluable in helping educators and therapists connect curriculum indicators to sensorimotor activities.

I would like to give special thanks to the wonderful teams of healthcare professionals, educators, and parents who attended my seminar workshop "Ready S.E.T. Go!" and contributed their lesson plans for this book:

Sakina Kapadia, Angie Kiddoo, Shalonda N. Williams, Lesley Kranz, MaryBeth Freitas, Cheryl Wascher, Tanya Lockwood, Kimberly Miller, Melissa Daniels, Michael Daniels, Caroline Radlinger, Jennifer Konieczny, Diane Bermann, Jean Imburgia, Becky Lossie, Christina Grey, Nancy LaFayette, Jennifer Brown, Ashley Goggans, Nicole Stoffel, Kristi Clark, Brenda Forslund, Kate Bennett, Jorie Hannan, Holly Sataloff, Kate Johnson, Kelly Mosley, Michelle Castiglioni, Kelly Blandy, Kim Sleep, Shelley Stroup, Kathy Miller, Janessa Manning, Iris Hamblin, Cathey Ivey, Linda Hamm, Jennifer Salter, Kay Ashida, Jamie McFadden, Beth Mosbach, Rachel Boxer, Jeff Gaschler, Laura Hatler, Jodi Frailing, Paula Johnson, Bill Bahnfleth, Ginger Boldt, Angie Roth, Sarah Patrickus, Maureen Mommaerts, Lisa Gross, Jennifer Cutler, Jean O'Flahrity, Sonja Bagley, Denise Wise, Linda Yates, Kori Vargas, Candi Adcock, Alan Amundson, Jennifer Harris, Diane Merlin, Loraine Ryan, Suzanne Cruz, Karen Steffens, TeriSue McEnery, Marjorie Swanson, Tisha DeGross, Lisa Loving, Gayle Pounds, Faith Rickert, Pam Hoffmann, Jennifer Landry, Suzette Howe, Barb Stiman, Susan M. Wilkinson, Lee Ann Lorenzon, S. Hanson, Renee Ades, Robin Schwab, Kay Nigbor, Leah Crull, Terri Steinhaus, Heidi Baumgartner, Tracy Boyer, Dianne Hendrickson, Jill Hermansen, Barbara Magera, Jackie Pederson, Lucky Peterson, Jessica Evenson, Kylie Long, Joyce Boo, Ellen Frankino, Sara Deitering, Heidi Larson, Anne Marie Johnson, Kriss Staab, Tricia Thorman, Heather Hough, Alanna Bosley, Erin Moser, Deb Moyer, Daphne Johnson, Karen Moe, Elisabeth Moe, Valerie Payne, Sari Micklewright, Lisa George, Nancy Morin, Sandi Halron, Helen

Kaiser, Jana Olson, Melissa Acker, Lisa Nikula, Nicole Giamos, Melissa Swedersky, Sally L. Hoftiezer, Lori Curtis, Shelley Hertz, and Mary McIntire-Belter.

I am also very appreciative of the written contribution by Debra Wilson on S'cool Moves, the written contribution and photos from Speed Stacks, Inc., the written contribution by Diana Henry on the Sensory Processing Measure, illustrations by Gerard Arantowicz, and photographs by Scott Campbell.

Finally, I would like to thank all of the children who so enthusiastically agreed to have their photos taken for the book: Jordan Wittbrod, Daniel Pauls, Derek Copeland, Alexandra Ginsberg, Daniel Spencer Clapp, Mistaya Spencer Clapp, Peggy Clark, Beckett Hutchinson, Wyatt Hutchinson, and Lauren Hess.

– Jenny Clark Brack

TABLE OF CONTENTS

FOREWORD xi

INTRODUCTION xiii

CHAPTER 1:
SENSORY PROCESSING DISORDER 1

Sensory Modulation Disorder 5
    Sensory Overresponsivity 5
    Sensory Underresponsivity 6
    Sensory Seeking..6
Sensory-Based Motor Disorder 7
    Dyspraxia..7
    Postural Disorder 7
Sensory Discrimination Disorder 8

CHAPTER 2:
EVIDENCE-BASED PRACTICE FOR CHILDREN WITH ASD AND SENSORY PROCESSING DISORDER..9

Brain Anatomy Differences in Children with ASD..10
Mirror Neurons 11
Animal-Assisted Therapy and ASD 13
Weighted Vests 15
    What the Research Says 15
Ball Chair 18
    What the Research Says 19
Disc 'O' Sit Cushion 19
    What the Research Says 20

CHAPTER 3:
ASSESSMENT AND EVALUATION 23

Response to Intervention (RtI)..23
Occupational Therapy and Collaboration 25
    Teacher Observation Checklist..26
Sensory Processing Measure 28
Sensory Profile School Companion 28
Writing Measurable Sensory Goals: Goal Attainment Scaling 29

CHAPTER 4: INTEGRATING ACTIVITY LESSON PLANS INTO ELEMENTARY SCHOOL ENVIRONMENTS 31

- Physical Education Class 34
  - Adaptive P.E. 34
- Recess – Outdoor/Indoor 35
  - Outdoor Recess 37
  - Indoor Recess 38
- Centers 38
- Imbedded into Curriculum 39
- After-School Therapeutic Playgroups/Clinic Settings 42
- Transitions 42

CHAPTER 5: LEARNING ENRICHMENTS 45

- Yoga for Kids 45
  - What the Research Says 46
- S'cool Moves 46
- Speed Stacks 47
  - What the Research Says 48
- The Influence of Music 48
  - What the Research Says 49
- Sign Language 50
- Quick Fixes 50
  - Sensory Activities to Alert the Brain for Learning 51
  - Modifications of Materials and Methods 52

LESSON THEMES 55

- Baseball 56
- Birthday Party 59
- Bugs 62
- Camping 66
- Car Wash 69
- Caterpillars 73
- Clouds 76
- Down on the Farm 79
- Fall Fun 83
- Fiesta! or Cinco De Mayo 86
- Finding Escaped Zoo Animals – Equestrian Therapy 88
- Flower Garden 90
- Football 93
- Fourth of July 96
- Garden 99
- Halloween 102

Insects 105
Laundry 109
Mardi Gras or 100th School Day 112
Outer Space 114
Pigs..116
Police 118
Puppies 121
Snow 124
Snowman...128
Spring Flowers 134
The Snowy Day...136
Vegetable Garden 139
Winter..142
Zoo 146

REFERENCES 151

APPENDIX 155
Teacher Observation Checklist..156
Adapted School Supply List 158
Definitions 160

PRODUCTS & RESOURCES 161

RECOMMENDED CHILDREN'S BOOKS 165

FOREWORD

Learn to Move, Moving Up! is an exceptional evidence-based resource for teachers, occupational therapists, parents, aides, or other individuals working with early-elementary children. Jenny's first successful book, *Learn to Move, Move to Learn!*, provides activity ideas for children in preschool and early childhood centers. As a next step, *Learn to Move, Moving Up!* presents from a sensory integration perspective a collection of activities for early-elementary children of all ability levels.

A unique feature of this book is that it provides a research foundation for sensory-based activities in a way that is easily understood. This is an exciting era, as research related to sensory integration and sensory processing disorders is growing, as highlighted by a complete issue of the *American Journal of Occupational Therapy* dedicated to research on sensory integration and sensory processing disorders in March/April 2007. Jenny cites many of the articles that were included in that issue, among other seminal research, to support the activities and concepts that she describes.

In addition, *Learn to Move, Moving Up!* provides valuable information about "best practices" in school settings. Response to Intervention (RtI), the general education initiative to facilitate high-quality education to all students, is discussed along with suggested methods for measuring progress, an essential element of RtI. Ideas for integrating the activity plans into the daily school schedule and curriculum, including adaptive P.E., recess, and classroom lessons, are also presented. The 30 themed activity plans address sensory, motor, language, academic, and social skills. The plans are well designed, ready to be used in a collaborative and inclusive manner within school settings.

Occupational therapists and other childhood specialists will find this a valuable resource. The book provides important background information in an-easy-to-understand format that is needed for evidence-based practice. Most important, the children will be the fortunate participants in fun and engaging sensorimotor learning experiences!

– *Patricia Davies, PhD, OTR, FAOTA*
Associate Professor, Colorado State University

INTRODUCTION

The transition from preschool to elementary school can be challenging for children with sensory processing difficulties as they struggle to adapt to new teachers, classrooms, friends, and academic expectations. One way to ensure a smooth changeover for children is by providing organized materials, reviewing routines, and having them meet new staff prior to the first day of school.

Structure and routine are essential for children with sensory processing disorder (SPD) to be successful academically and enjoy their elementary education. This book presents 30 structured sensorimotor theme-based lesson plans along with literacy and curriculum suggestions. The curriculum suggestions provide educators with extension activities that allow them to expand learned concepts using multisensory teaching methods.

To create a context for the lesson plans, the book also includes an overview of sensory processing, evidence-based practice options, sensory deficits and children on the autism spectrum, creative suggestions for implementing lesson plans in elementary school environments, information about yoga, S'cool Moves, Speed Stacks, music therapy, sign language, quick fixes for the classroom, and assessment/evaluation tools for collaborative decision making.

The lesson plans follow the same structure and philosophy as those in my first book, *Learn to Move, Move to Learn – Sensorimotor Early Childhood Activity Themes* (Brack, 2004) for early childhood environments. It is my hope that the timely material in this book will prove valuable to professionals working with elementary school-age children and, ultimately, help improve children's lives.

– *Jenny Clark Brack*

CHAPTER 1

SENSORY PROCESSING DISORDER

Christopher is crying and covering his ears with his hands while hiding under his desk. The class just came inside from recess. Lucy, one of the other students, tells the teacher what happened on the playground.

Christopher is standing near the sandbox and Joseph accidentally throws sand on him. Christopher does not like the texture of sand and becomes very upset, pushing Joseph and calling him names. The playground supervisor catches Christopher's behavior and puts him in time-out. When it is time to line up to go inside, Christopher is standing in the middle of the line when Larry, who is standing behind him, accidentally bumps into him. Christopher thinks Larry is purposefully hurting him and turns around to hit him. The teacher observes Christopher's behavior, and he gets in trouble again.

As the students enter the classroom, they are talking loudly and excitedly. Due to his sensitivity to loud sounds, Christopher immediately runs over and hides under his desk, covering his ears in an attempt to calm the world around him. It takes a whole 10 minutes for Christopher to calm down so he can even begin to feel ready to listen and learn. Even so, he is so upset that he has trouble focusing on the teacher's instructions and, as a result, he recalls very little information for the classroom assignment.

To the uninformed, Christopher's behavior seems unpredictable and irrational. As a result, he not only attracts negative teacher attention and suffers the consequences, but his ability to learn is impacted. All this is due to his sensory processing disorder (SPD).

SPD is a neurological condition that interferes with the daily lives of approximately 1 in 20 children (Ahn, Miller, Milberger, & McIntosh, 2004). SPD occurs when the brain inaccurately perceives sensation from touch, sight, sound, smell, and movement. Many people experience occasional difficulties processing sensation, such as not being able to tolerate loud sounds when having a headache or being bothered by tags in their clothing.

Children with SPD, however, experience significant and chronic symptoms that can disrupt daily living activities and negatively affect their participation in everyday life. For example, a child with SPD not only cannot tolerate tags in his clothing, he may have emotional meltdowns from the texture of sock seams, certain types of clothing materials, toothbrush bristles, food textures, art media, and having his fingernails cut. These symptoms are a daily occurrence and impact food choices, hygiene, participation in school activities, and social interactions.

Sensory Integration

The concept of sensory processing disorder has its roots in sensory integration theory, developed in the 1970s by Jean Ayres. Dr. Ayres earned BS and MA degrees in occupational therapy and a Ph.D. in educational psychology from the University of Southern California. She completed a post-doctoral traineeship at the UCLA Brain Research Institute under Dr. Arther Parmelee. In addition to her occupational therapy credentials, Dr. Ayres was also a California licensed psychologist.

Ayres defined sensory integration as "the neurological process that organizes sensation from one's own body and from the environment and makes it possible to use the body effectively within the environment" (Ayres, 1979, p. 11). In other words, sensory integration allows us to participate in daily activities and experience sensations such as the taste of a hotdog, the feel of clothing textures, the sounds of birds while playing in the park, and the movement from riding a bicycle.

Children who have difficulty with sensory processing experience sensory input as confusing, upsetting, or not meaningful. For example, at school during a fire drill when the fire alarm sounds, a child reacts by covering her ears, becomes upset and cries, and has difficulty re-engaging in the task at hand. At home, a child avoids brushing his teeth because the toothbrush texture does not feel good in his mouth. In the community, a child steers clear of playground equipment because he is afraid of heights.

Certain types of sensation, especially in new environments, can be so overwhelming for a child that her emotional reactions present as willful behavior to others. Such rigid and controlling behavior impacts social interactions with others and interferes with engaging in everyday activities.

A child attending a typical birthday party experiences a wealth of sensory input: the sounds of all the children talking, singing, and blowing of horns; the sights of balloons, gifts, and candles; the sensation of other children accidentally bumping into him; the texture of the elastic string under his chin from the birthday hat; and the taste, texture, and temperature of the cake and ice-cream.

A typical child is able to take in all the sensations – usually without even being aware of them – and have an enjoyable time. A child with SPD, on the other hand, may experience the sounds as too loud and the sights as overwhelming. The tactile sensation of children accidentally bumping into him may disrupt his personal boundary space, leading him to misinterpret the sensation as purposefully hurtful. Finally, he may not like the texture of the chocolate cake or the coldness of the ice cream.

In an effort to cope with these uncomfortable and sometimes painful sensations, the child may shut down or lash out. Not surprising, such behavior can negatively impact social interaction with people around him. This example illustrates only one type of sensory processing pattern; there is a broad spectrum of processing patterns, from sensory sensitive to sensory underresponsive, with various symptoms across developmental age groups of children. (Refer to Chapter 3, Assessment and

Evaluation, for suggestions on how to identify children with sensory difficulties in preparation for choosing the most effective intervention strategy.)

It is important to accurately categorize a child's sensory processing patterns in order to develop treatment plans that target the child's needs. Miller, Anzalone, Lane, Cermak, and Osten (2007) have suggested that SPD be divided into three patterns, each with subtypes, as follows.*

1. **Sensory modulation disorder**
   a. Sensory overresponsivity
   b. Sensory underresponsivity
   c. Sensory seeking
2. **Sensory-based motor disorder**
   a. Dyspraxia
   b. Postural disorder
3. **Sensory discrimination disorder**
   a. Visual
   b. Auditory
   c. Tactile
   d. Vestibular
   e. Proprioception
   f. Taste/smell

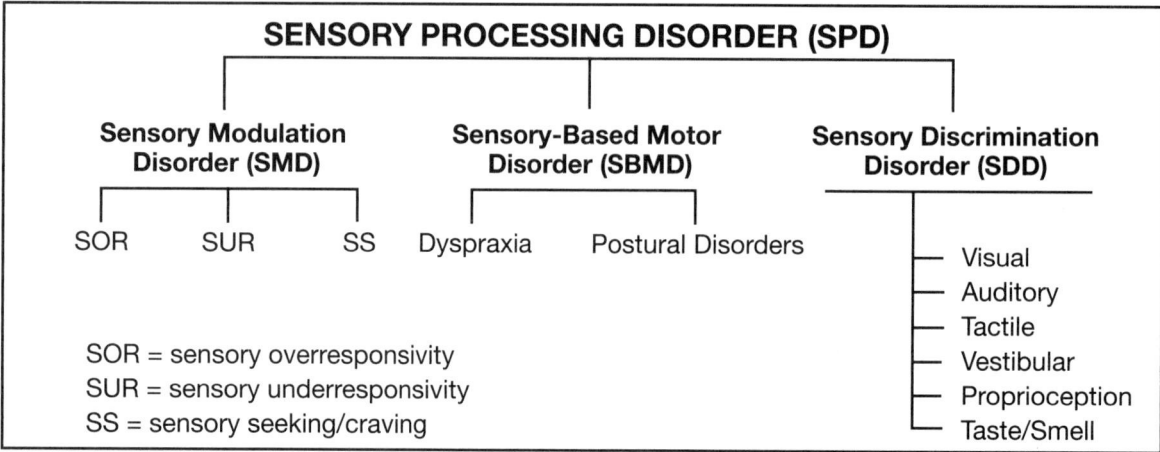

Figure 1. A proposed new nosology for sensory processing disorder.

Miller, L. J., Anzalone M. E., Lane, S. J., Cermak, S. A., & Osten, E. T. (2007). Concept evolution in sensory integration: A proposed nosology for diagnosis. *American Journal of Occupational Therapy, 61*(2), p. 137. Reprinted with permission.

In the following, we will take a closer look at SPD using Miller et al.'s classification.

---

* Miller, Anzalone, Lane, Cermak, and Osten have submitted a proposal for diagnostic classification of SPD, with the ultimate goal of including SPD in the 2012 revision of the *Diagnostic and Statistical Manual of Mental Disorders IV-TR* (DSM) by the American Psychiatric Association.

SENSORY MODULATION DISORDER

> **Sensory Modulation**
>
> *Sensory Modulation Disorder* (SMD) is a problem with turning sensory messages into controlled behaviors that match the nature and intensity of the sensory information" (Miller & Fuller, 2006, p. 12). Modulation occurs every moment of our day, allowing us to focus on important input, while ignoring irrelevant input. Modulation takes place at an unconscious level such that most of us are unaware of the small adjustments our nervous system makes to help us participate smoothly in daily life activities.
>
> When input is not properly modulated, it can affect the ability to attend to task. For example, if a teacher is giving instructions for a math assignment, the child who has poor modulation may have difficulty tuning out extraneous background sounds, such as children's voices in the hallway or the noise from the heater, be distracted by them, and consequently miss the point of the instructions.

"We hall have sensory preferences, yet students with sensory modulation disorder have very strong sensory likes and dislikes and their reaction to sensory input departs from typical expected responses. Their responses can be manifested as overresponsivity and/or sensory seeking behaviors" (Henry, Kane-Wineland, & Swindeman, 2007, p. 4).

Sensory Overresponsivity

Sensory overresponsivity is also commonly referred to as sensory defensiveness. Sensory defensiveness (Wilbarger & Wilbarger, 1991) can occur in more than one sensory system and involves a "fight, flight, or freeze" reaction. When a sensory defensive reaction occurs, the autonomic nervous system (ANS), which regulates heart rate, respiration, and digestion, releases adrenaline and cortisol. This is intended to assist us in preparing to protect our bodies from harm, and is useful when there is a real threat. For example, if you are driving down the road and a deer jumps out in front of your car, your ANS works instantly, allowing you to react quickly by putting the brakes on or maneuvering your car out of the way to be safe.

In children who have sensory defensiveness, their ANS responds to typical everyday events in the same manner, even if not called for. For example, a child who is auditorily defensive – has a low neurological threshold to sound – may go into a "fight, flight, or freeze" reaction when a school bell sounds because his ANS identifies the bell as a potential threat. As a result, she may run out of the classroom or hit the child sitting next to her. If teachers, parents, and others are unaware of the child's sensory sensitivity to sound, such behavior will not make sense. As a result, they may discipline the child rather than problem solve and develop sensory strategies and accommodations that possibly will prevent future occurrences.

Sensory Underresponsivity

Another subtype of SMD is sensory underresponsivity. Children with sensory underresponsivity require intense sensory input to notice sensations and lack initial awareness of stimuli. These children tend to have decreased sensory registration, defined as "the initial awareness of a sensation" (Williamson & Anzalone, 2001, p. 13). Thus, in order to notice a new sensation in her environment, such as a change in temperature, sound, or lighting, the child has to become aware of the new stimulus before she can attend to it. Children with underresponsivity appear to be sedentary, lethargic, and apathetic, and they tend to lack an inner drive, be withdrawn, and may take longer to respond. Such children are often mislabeled as "lazy" or "unmotivated" (Miller et al., 2007).

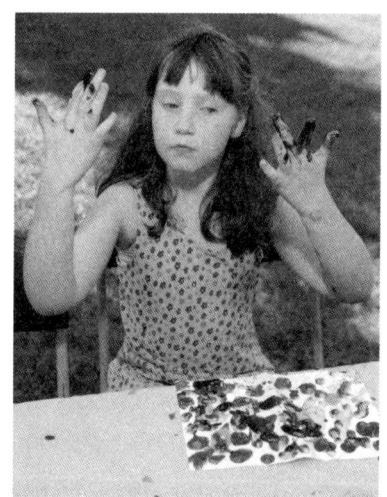

Children with autism spectrum disorder (ASD), a major focus of this book, fall into both categories of over- and underresponsivity in multiple sensory systems (Tomchek & Dunn, 2007). For example, a child may demonstrate poor tolerance for tactile sensation such as getting paint on her fingers in art or having her hair or nails cut (overresponsivity), but may need to feel the heavy sensation of a weighted blanket to calm for sleeping (underresponsivity).

Sensory Seeking

A third subtype of SMD is sensory seeking. Children who are sensory seeking prefer intense and extreme sensory input. These children may be viewed as "dare devils," who prefer to rock climb or go fast on the merry-go-round. They may not easily feel pain or make sounds with their mouth as a way to stimulate their auditory system, and they often play roughly with toys and other children. The consequence of such behavior is poor impulse control, leading to physical contact that can harm another individual or the child himself.

SENSORY-BASED MOTOR DISORDER

Sensory-based motor disorders are divided into two subtypes: dyspraxia and postural disorder.

Dyspraxia

The term *dyspraxia* (sometimes called Developmental Coordination Disorder: DCD) comes from the word *praxis*, which refers to paying conscious attention to a task while relying on stored sensory information from each of the sensory systems. For example, adults snow skiing for the first time rely on the sense of vision to navigate around obstacles, hearing to listen to instructions, tactile sensations to feel the ski boots and ski poles, and movement sensations to learn the new skill of snow skiing. While relying on sensations of which they are not consciously aware, they learn the motor patterns by consciously focusing on manipulating the skis and the poles to perform the motions with smooth movements.

Dyspraxia, in contrast, refers to difficulty in executing unfamiliar motor actions, affecting oral, fine- and gross-motor coordination. Children with dyspraxia have poor awareness of their body in space, thus displaying symptoms such as bumping into other people or objects, poor articulation, illegible handwriting, and awkward motor skills in physical education class as well as sports. Children with dyspraxia need excessive repetition to learn new motor skill and have to cognitively "think" about how to move their bodies.

Postural Disorder

Postural disorder is described as "difficulty stabilizing the body during movement or at rest to meet the demands of the environment or of a given motor task" (Miller et al., 2007, p. 138). Thus, it is characterized by poor motor control, poor stability, or poor balance due to an imbalance in muscle tone (hypertonic – high muscle tone or hypotonic – low muscle tone). Children with poor postural control have difficulty with movement against gravity and may slump at their desk or fall out of their chair.

SENSORY DISCRIMINATION DISORDER

Sensory discrimination disorder involves difficulty perceiving the details of sensation to identify differences or similarities. Poor discrimination can occur in one or more sensory systems. Ultimately, a child's learning, self-esteem, and behavior are impacted by a sensory discrimination disorder, as extra time is required to process information. For example, a child with poor visual discrimination may have difficulty discerning "b" from "d" and, therefore, struggle with reading. He may be very much aware that his peers are reading more fluently than he is, which affects his self-confidence and his sense of "fitting in." This, in turn, may cause him to display inappropriate behaviors in the classroom and act out as the "class clown" to hide his difficulties and try to be accepted by his peers.

Table 1.1 Examples of Discrimination Disorder

• Poor auditory discrimination
  – Trouble discerning speech sounds
  – Demonstrates delays with processing verbal directions 

• Poor tactile discrimination
  – Difficulty manipulating fasteners unless looking at them
  – May not notice food on face after eating 

• Poor discrimination with movement (vestibular)   – Difficulty with balance tasks such as navigating stairs 

• Poor discrimination with muscles (proprioception)
  – May misjudge the amount of pressure to use when coloring, consequently breaking crayons
  – Trouble judging body space and bump into objects 

• Decreased taste/smell discrimination     – May be particular about food choices

Note. *Sensory Gang* ©Autism Asperger Publishing Company. Used with permission.

As illustrated, children with SPD struggle with participating in daily activities and routines at school, at home, and in the community. These children need emotional support and physical accommodations to experience success in all environments. Chapter 2 will examine how SPD affects children on the autism spectrum, as well as present some evidence-based interventions that address sensory needs.

CHAPTER 2

EVIDENCE-BASED PRACTICE FOR CHILDREN WITH ASD AND SENSORY PROCESSING DISORDER

In this chapter we will discuss brain differences in children with autism spectrum disorders (ASD) and how they impact sensory processing patterns that affect participation and engagement in daily tasks. Chapter 2 will also review the research supporting two so-called evidence-based practices, weighted vests and dynamic seating options, including ball chairs and Disc 'O' Sit cushions. The focus will be on the benefits of these interventions for attaining engagement, attention to task, and in-seat behavior – all important for preparing children to learn and to function smoothly in their daily lives at school, at home, and in the community.

BRAIN ANATOMY DIFFERENCES IN CHILDREN WITH ASD

Children with ASD struggle in school settings due to social and language delays as well as sensory and motor skill deficits. Functional activities such as handwriting, shoe tying, cutting, eating, playing a musical instrument, and participating in physical education can be very challenging. In addition, difficulty tolerating the loud noise level of the cafeteria or gymnasium, the texture of art materials, or the need for excessive movement can interfere with school success.

Why do many children with ASD have these challenges? Current research on the brain functioning of these children may help answer this question.

It has recently been discovered that children with ASD have unusual differences in the anatomy of their brain compared to their neurotypical peers. That is, researchers at Johns Hopkins (Wallace, 2006) have discovered that the brains of children with ASD show perplexing signs of inflammation from excess white matter, causing their brain size to be larger than normal. Further, using magnetic resonance imaging (MRI) and tape measure readings, researchers at Children's Hospital in San Diego discovered that children with ASD experience rapid brain expansion by age 2, and by age 4 their brains are the size of a 13-year-old's. This inflammation is most notable in the frontal lobes, the part of the brain that is responsible for higher reasoning (Wallace, 2006) (see Figure 2.1).

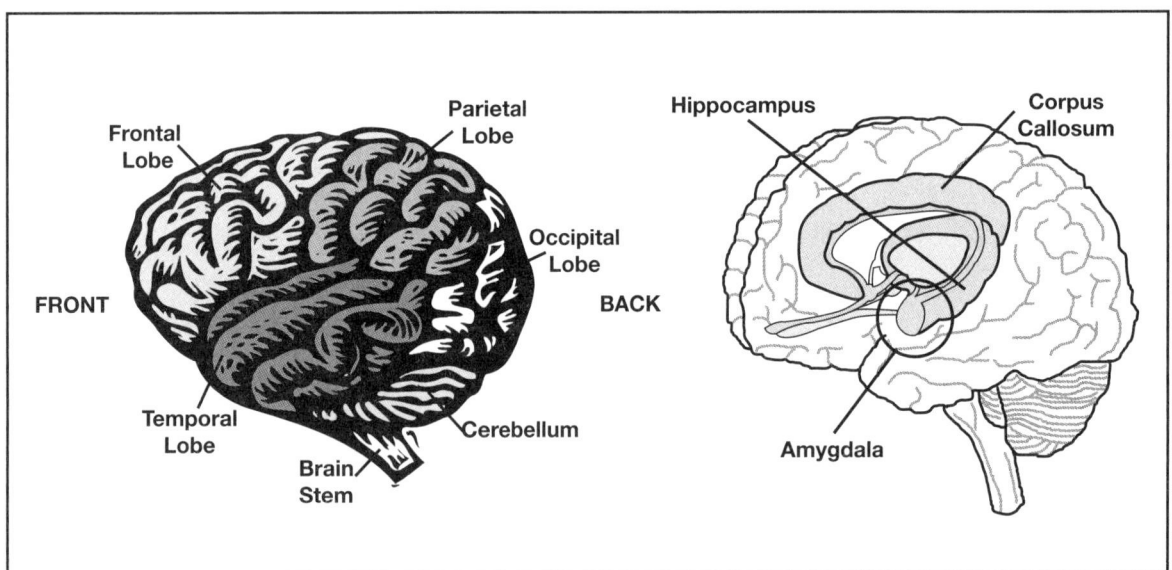

Figure 2.1. Components of typical brain.

The amygdala also shows signs of inflammation (Wallace, 2006). Given that the amygdala is the gateway to the emotion-regulating system and contributes to social behavior, enlargement of the amygdala may explain why many children with ASD demonstrate high levels of anxiety. Further, the amygdala is activated when looking at faces, which may be one reason why children with ASD avoid eye contact.

The corpus callosum, located between the right and left hemispheres of the brain (see Figure 2.1), is responsible for transferring neural communication between both halves of the brain. In children with ASD, the corpus callosum is undersized, creating poor neural coordination across different areas of the brain, which has an effect on language.

The hippocampus, in turn, plays a primary role in memory processes, especially the formation of new memory. In children with ASD, brain imaging has shown that the hippocampus appears to be slightly larger than normal. Williams, Goldstein, and Minshew (2006) found that children with ASD have poor memory for complex visual and verbal information with intact verbal working memory and recognition memory. Children with ASD use these types of memory to interpret cognitive functions that neurotypical children process in other regions of the brain, which may explain why the hippocampus is enlarged in the brains of children with ASD.

Finally, the cerebellum, located in the back of the brain, functions to ensure smooth, coordinated motor skills and motor planning of newly learned motor skills. Courchesne (2006, cited in Wallis, 2006) found that that this region is overloaded with white matter in the brains of children with ASD. This could explain why 50%-90% of children with ASD have problems with motor coordination, including balance, bilateral coordination, body awareness in surrounding space, and fine-motor skills.

MIRROR NEURONS

Studies in the early 1990s revealed a unique set of nerve cells, mirror neurons, that are involved with social interaction, empathy, and learning (Rizzolati, Fogassi, & Gallese, 2006). When we perform an action, the mirror mechanism allows an observer to understand physiologically what we are doing by experiencing it first in his own mind. This, in turn, allows the observer to evaluate our actions and intentions and thus empathize and respond in a socially appropriate manner. For example, a mother slices an apple into several pieces while her child is standing nearby watching. The child observes his mother and concludes that he will soon be fed and, therefore, reaches toward his mother to accept the apple slices. Researchers at University of California San Diego discovered that people with ASD have reduced mirror neuron activity in several regions of the brain, which may explain some of the symptoms of autism such as lack of empathy and social isolation (Ramachandran & Oberman, 2006).

Forty percent of children with ASD have sensory sensitivity to touch, sound, taste, light, and smell, as well as sensory underresponsivity to vestibular, proprioceptive, and tactile input (Rimland, 1990). To explain these sensory processing difficulties, Ramachandran and Oberman (2006) proposed the salience landscape theory, as follows. In a typical child, sensory input is transferred to the amygdala, which, as we have seen, regulates emotions. Using stored information obtained from the mirror neurons, the amygdala provides the child with a template based on which she can respond emotionally to a particular event or situation, creating the so-called salience landscape. This response is unique to each situation whether it is a fearful event (confronting a wild animal), a loving event (hugging a parent), or a trivial event (riding in a car).

Children with ASD respond to trivial incidents with extreme emotions, presumably because the connections between the sensory areas and the amygdala are distorted. For example, a typical child eats lunch in the school cafeteria and socializes with his friends talking, laughing, and eating with no regard to the loud, busy environment around him. A child with ASD, however, may be so overwhelmed with the loud sounds, the smells from the food, and the large number of children that he covers his ears, screams to drown out the sounds, and hides under the lunch table to escape.

Tomchek and Dunn (2007) used the Short Sensory Profile to investigate differences in sensory processing between children with ASD and same-aged typically developing peers. Specifically, they compared the sensory processing abilities of 281 children with ASD to those of age-matched typically developing peers. Results were significant, indicating that 95% of the children with ASD had sensory processing differences on the total score of the Short Sensory Profile compared to peers. The most significant areas of difference were noted in subsections of Underresponsive/Seeks Sensation, Auditory Filtering, and Tactile Sensitivity. These findings contribute to validating the pervasiveness of sensory processing impairments in children with ASD.

Understanding the sensory characteristics of children with ASD can lead teachers, therapists, and parents toward effective interventions. While interventions are unique to each child for individual situations, some interventions have been shown specifically to be beneficial to children with ASD.

Animal-Assisted Therapy and ASD

Research (Sams, Fortney, & Willenberg, 2006) has shown that the use of animals is powerful in helping children with ASD develop social and communication skills. Animal-assisted therapy involves using animals, such as horses for therapeutic horseback riding, trained therapy dogs, personal pets such as cats, or other animals like llamas and rabbits to promote improvement in human physical, emotional, social, and cognitive functioning. Sams et al. compared language and social interactions between children with ASD receiving standard occupational therapy techniques, such as cutting, catching a ball, or swinging, and children with ASD receiving the same therapy but with animals incorporated. The latter demonstrated a significantly greater use of language and social interactions.

In a single-case study, Barol, a graduate student in New Mexico Highland University School of Social Work (Barol, 2007), investigated if animal-assisted therapy increased social skills. A 5-year-old child with ASD was observed while engaged in therapy sessions with a specially trained dog. Results were encouraging as the child, who was nonverbal prior to the study, spoke his first sentence part way through the study. In addition, the child began to make social interactions with the therapists and became more aware of others' needs by offering snacks to therapists.

Examining the effectiveness of occupational therapy and sensory integration with children on the autism spectrum, Baranek (2002) found improved play skills, social interaction, adult interaction, and approach to motor tasks, as well as a decrease in sensory sensitivities. No changes were noted in interactions with peers, however.

Children with ASD will be better able to modulate their nervous systems to a attain and maintain a focused state of alertness, improve motor coordination, increase self-esteem through success, and acquire social skills, prevocational, academic, and play skills when a combination of sensory integration therapy, sensory strategies in the environment, and a sensory diet (sensory activities and sensory modifications incorporated into daily routines) are implemented. Sensory diets for children with ASD and SPD consist of choosing effective therapeutic products and interventions. Using evidence-based choices is imperative for creating successful conditions for children with ASD and SPD.

> **Case Example**
>
> Jack, a 7-year-old boy with autism, demonstrates difficulty with sensory modulation as well as decreased muscle strength and coordination. These delays negatively impact his handwriting, physical education skills, social interactions with peers, and engagement throughout his daily routines both at home and school.
>
> Jack receives occupational therapy (OT) services in a clinic and at school. In his weekly clinic OT sessions, he engages in movement activities such as swinging and rolling and heavy work activities such as jumping and crawling through an obstacle course. These activities stimulate his underlying sensory systems for attaining and maintaining a state of modulated alertness, which improves his ability to sustain focus on functional tasks, increases his motivation, and improves his behavior by decreasing his anxiety.
>
> In addition, the clinic OT collaborates with the parents and provides suggestions to help Jack at home and in the community with behavioral and social needs that may arise. The school OT helps Jack by collaborating with school staff regarding his sensory needs in the educational environment. Jack wears a weighted vest (see page 15) intermittently during the school day, which helps him to stay on task and be engaged. In addition, the school OT provides recommendations for Jack's handwriting needs, such as using adapted handwriting paper, a pencil grip, and a slanted surface on which to write for improved view of his paper and physical support of his arm. The school OT also consults with Jack's teachers regarding participation needs that may arise at school, such as in music class, physical education class, at recess or lunch.
>
> After six months of OT at the clinic and in the school setting, Jack is finding increasing success in school with academics, peer social interactions and involvement in extracurricular activities, and improved sensory self-regulation, which empowers him to advocate for his personal needs – a significant lifelong goal.

Making decisions for therapeutic interventions for children with ASD and SPD in school settings requires creativity, resourcefulness, and teamwork. It is important to stay current on best practice techniques and research on sensory processing so that children receive optimal therapeutic interventions. Evidence can be obtained from a variety of sources, including reviewing professional research journals, such as *American Journal of Occupational Therapy*, surfing the web on sites such as www.pubmedcentral.com, at the U.S. National Institutes of Health (NIH), developed and managed by NIH's National Center for Biotechnology Information (NCBI) in the National Library of Medicine (NLM), and collecting data specific to a given child and situation.

Let's take a look at a few therapeutic products commonly implemented as interventions for children with ASD and SPD – weighted vest, ball chair, and Disc O' Sit cushion.

WEIGHTED VESTS

One therapeutic intervention used in schools and in the community for children with sensory processing and attention difficulties is the use of a weighted vest. The proprioceptive, deep-pressure touch input obtained from wearing a weighted vest provides a calming and organizing effect by stimulating an increase in neurotransmitters – chemical substances such as serotonin, norepinephrine, and epinephrine – that transmit information from one nerve cell to another. Increased numbers of neurotransmitters available to the brain increase the level of arousal in the nervous system, thereby improving the ability to attend to task.

A student can wear a weighted vest while engaging in functional activities throughout the school day. The vest can be worn over clothing and can appear as typical clothing if trendy material is used to make the vest, making the child blend in with peers. Teachers can easily implement the use of a weighted vest under the direction of an occupational therapist.

What the Research Says
Time on Task
VandenBerg (2001) studied the effects of wearing a weighted vest to improve the on-task behavior of children with attention deficit-hyperactivity disorder (ADHD). VandenBerg hypothesized that the deep-pressure touch input from the weighted vest would affect the limbic system, the part of the brain that regulates emotion and behavior, and stimulate production of neurotransmitters, which modulate arousal levels, similarly to some medications, ultimately producing a calming effect and increasing attention.

Four students with ADHD were timed to measure on-task behavior during fine-motor tasks for six 15-minute observations while wearing the weighted vest and six 15-minute observations with no weighted vest. Results showed that on-task behavior increased by 18%-25% in all four students while they were wearing the weighted vest.

Attention to Task and Self-Stimulatory Behavior

Children on the autism spectrum tend to display self-stimulatory behaviors as a way to calm when they are agitated. Some of these behaviors seek sensation that provides deep-pressure touch input, such as toe walking, tapping, and arm flapping.

Fertel-Daly, Bedell, and Hinojosa (2001) examined the use of a weighted vest in five preschoolers with pervasive developmental disorders, including a child with autism. Specifically, the authors examined the effectiveness of the weighted vest on improving attention to task with fine-motor activities and decreasing self-stimulatory behaviors. Five children wore the weighted vest as follows: on for 2 hours and off for 2 hours.

Results were positive, showing that all five participants demonstrated a decrease in the number of distractions and an increase in attention while wearing the weighted vest. All but one also displayed a decrease in self-stimulatory behaviors while wearing the vest.

Two commonly asked questions regarding using weighted vests as a therapeutic tool are:
1. What is the appropriate wearing schedule?
2. How much weight should be used in the vest?

Wearing Schedule

Fertel-Daly et al. (2001) addressed wearing schedules. Occupational therapists commonly recommend that weighted vests be worn for 20 minutes on and 1-1/2-2 hours off. Since proprioceptive (deep pressure/heavy work) input has an effect for up to 2 hours, the off time is indisputable. Fertel-Daly et al. found that wearing the weighted vest for up to 2 hours had a positive impact on increasing attention, decreasing distractions, and decreasing self-stimulatory behaviors.

Best practice involves examination of the evidence when deciding on an appropriate wearing schedule. Data collection through observation of response to different lengths of wearing time that is specific to a child is necessary to determine how a given child will respond to a particular wearing schedule. It is important to note that the nervous system responds to change in sensory input. If the weighted vest is worn continuously throughout the day, a child's nervous system may habituate, that is, get used to the sensation, and as a result no longer profit from the effect of the weighted vest. Therefore, the weighted vest is only beneficial if worn alternately on for a period of time and off for a period of time throughout the day.

Optimal Weight

To address the question regarding optimal weight used in the vest to achieve a therapeutic outcome – increased attention and on-task behavior – therapists may review the literature for supportive evidence and collect data through observation of a child's response to different amounts of weight. Based on substantiation from practicing occupational therapists combined with research results, Vandenberg (2001) noted that 5% of a child's body weight is the ideal therapeutic weight for weighted vests. Thus, for example, if the child weights 50 lbs, the weight of the vest would be 2-1/2 lbs.

Honaker and Rossi (2005) designed a protocol CAT (Critically Appraised Topics) Brief to analyze evidence from published literature, surveys, interviews, and expert opinions on the amount of weight needed for effectiveness in terms of improved attention and engagement during the school day. Evidence from the CAT Brief consistently found that the beneficial amount of weight used in a weighted vest is, on average, 5% of a child's body weight.

Although research on proprioceptive input is limited to weighted vests, there are many other ways to obtain deep-pressure touch input for calming and organizing. Some of them are inexpensive and easy to implement, as illustrated in Table 2.1.

Table 2.1
Other Ways to Receive Proprioceptive Input

- Weighted lap bag (sew a rectangular piece of material into columns and stuff with rice, beans, fish tank rocks, etc.)
- Beanbag chair
- Pressure garments
  Examples:
  - *Bear Hugs Pressure Vest* (made from neoprene material, worn over clothing, fastens with Velcro; may be purchased from www.Southpawenterprises.com).
  - *Under Armour compression-fit clothing* (made from breathable stretch fabric, worn under clothing or as clothing; may be purchased from www.under-armour.com or at a sporting goods store)
  - *SPIO Stabilizing Pressure Input Orthosis* (made from lightweight breathable fabric, worn under clothing, available as a vest, shirt, pants, unitard, or gloves; may be purchased from www.spioworks.com)
- Chair push-ups and pull-ups
- Heavy jobs at school, such as carrying library books, milk cartons, putting chairs on desks, etc.

BALL CHAIR

Another common therapeutic intervention that helps some students stay in their seat for longer periods of time in order to complete schoolwork is the use of a ball chair for added movement input. Children with underresponsive vestibular systems (those who need increased sensation to notice and respond) need excessive movement to attain and maintain attention to task. The use of a therapy ball as a chair can provide this input (Schilling, Washington, Billingsley, & Deitz, 2003). The evidence on page 19 indicates the efficacy of using a therapy ball in place of a regular chair for some children.

What the Research Says

Time in Seat and Legible Word Productivity — Students with ADHD

Schilling et al. (2003) compared the effects of using a therapy ball chair versus a regular chair in the classroom. Specifically, they investigated whether the movement provided from sitting on a therapy ball chair helped children with ADHD stay in their seats for longer periods of time and whether sitting on a therapy ball chair had an effect on legible word productivity.

Three students with ADHD were chosen for the 12-week study. Data were collected within a fourth-grade inclusive classroom and during language arts. Results were favorable: All three participants improved their in-seat behavior and increased legible word productivity when sitting on the therapy ball chair. In addition, the students made comments inferring a preference for the therapy ball chair, such as "You can keep your brain active even when you're bored."

Engagement, Active Participation in Functional Tasks, Social Interactions, and Attention — Students with ASD

Another study examined the effects of using a therapy ball chair with children on the autism spectrum. Children with ASD display behaviors such as difficulty initiating engagement, difficulty with active participation in functional tasks, socially inappropriate interactions, and decreased attention. Schilling and Schwartz (2004) examined four preschool children with ASD to determine the effect of using a therapy ball chair in the classroom on their in-seat behavior and engagement.

Results were remarkable, showing improvements in engagement and in-seat behavior when the children were sitting on the therapy ball chairs. In addition, teachers reported that the children preferred the therapy ball chairs to other seating options such as regular chairs or carpet squares. These findings suggest that the use of therapy balls as chairs can improve engagement and in-seat behavior and help children with ASD attain and maintain a focused state of alertness for listening to instruction and completing tasks.

DISC 'O' SIT CUSHION

While evidence on the use of a ball chair to improve attention to task has been documented in the past, more recently Pfeiffer, Henry, Miller, and Witherell (2008) investigated the use of a Disc 'O' Sit cushion for improving attention to task with second-grade students. A Disc 'O' Sit cushion is a round air-filled plastic cushion manufactured by Gymnic (www.gymnic.com), Osoppo, Italy.

What the Research Says
Attention in Academic Settings

Participants in this study included 63 second-grade students identified with attention difficulties in the academic setting. The Behavioral Rating Inventory of Executive Function (BRIEF; Gioia, Isquith, Guy, & Kenworthy, 1996) was completed by the classroom teachers and used for pretest and posttest measurements of student behavior. Thirty-one students were assigned to the treatment group and 32 students to the control group. Participants from the treatment group sat on the Disc 'O' Sit cushion, which was placed on a regular classroom chair, throughout the school day for two weeks. Participants from the control group sat on regular classroom chairs for two weeks without the cushion.

Pfeiffer et al. (2008) found a significant difference in attention to task after the Disc 'O' Sit cushion intervention and a significant difference between the control group and treatment group. Specifically, the treatment group showed an increase in attention as measured by the BRIEF.

Although research on dynamic seating is limited to therapy ball chairs and Disc 'O' Sit cushions, there are many other ways to obtain vestibular sensory input. Some options are inexpensive and easy to implement. Table 2.2 lists a few examples.

Table 2.2
Other Ways to Obtain Vestibular Sensory Input

- Partially inflated beach ball
- Partially inflated camping pillow
- Cutting slits in two tennis balls and placing them on diagonal corners of chair legs
- Movin' Sit cushion (www.abilitations.com)
- Allowing students to stand at their desk

Levine and his colleagues have developed a "classroom of the future" that uses increased activity coinciding with learning (Puliti, 2007). This unconventional concept involves chairless classrooms. In addition, desks are replaced with adjustable podiums, allowing the students to learn while standing, kneeling, or sitting on therapy ball chairs. Currently, over 20 schools are participating in a study of the effects on student learning of this model.

In addition to the evidence-based interventions commonly used by occupational therapists to address sensory processing difficulties in school settings discussed here, many other creative strategies, accommodations, and adaptations can assist in achieving successful school performance. Struggling students must be observed and assessed to determine which interventions are most appropriate.

Chapter 2 reviewed some of the unique challenges children with ASD face with sensory processing difficulties on a daily basis, including integration with peers into school environments and activities. It also examined some evidence-based interventions that can be implemented into school settings to enhance school success. Chapter 3 will look at some assessment options for identifying students with sensory processing difficulties and examine how these difficulties impact educational progress. In addition, Chapter 3 will review response to intervention (RtI) for implementing pertinent school strategies, as well as the importance of collaboration for decision-making regarding appropriate interventions.

CHAPTER 3

ASSESSMENT AND EVALUATION

Identifying a student's educational needs involves observing the student in various school environments, noting areas of concern, and collaborating with school staff regarding strategies to help the student achieve successful school performance. Collaboration brings teams of professionals together to unite expertise, knowledge, and perspective in order to make educational decisions.

This chapter discusses assessment, beginning with the role of response to intervention (RtI). It also examines the importance of team collaboration for making educational decisions, reviews two standardized sensory evaluations, and looks at developing measurable sensory goals for evaluating educational progress.

RESPONSE TO INTERVENTION (RtI)

Response to intervention, a general education initiative, is defined as "the practice of (1) providing high-quality instruction/intervention matched to student needs, and (2) using learning rate over time and level of performance to (3) make important education decisions" (Batsch, Elliott, Graden, Grimes, Kovaleski, Prasse et al., 2006, p. 2). RtI is an opportunity for general education and special education staff to collaborate, allowing for a more cohesive system of education and making everyone accountable for student learning.

RtI involves monitoring struggling general education students and their progress with regard to selected interventions and using special education as a strategy when general education interventions are not effective for a given student. RtI emphasizes early intervening, evidence-based decision making, and data collection to guide interventions. This format allows flexibility with regard to a student's unique circumstance, as well as creativity with regard to altering the curriculum as needed for students to meet curriculum indicators.

RtI involves three levels (Tiers), and students may move between Tiers depending on the level of intervention they need. Tier I focuses on whole-group interventions for all students and is considered both proactive and preventive. Tier II interventions serve approximately 15% of the students considered at risk and focus on group interventions. At this level, special education staff may be involved in providing suggestions for modifications of materials and methods. Finally, Tier III interventions serve approximately 5% of students. At this level, students receive intensive and individual intervention. Special education staff may be involved to observe a child in a variety of school environments and provide very specific suggestions for accommodations, modifications, and adaptations with more frequent follow-up, and determine if there is a need to refer for a comprehensive special education evaluation.

ACADEMIC SYSTEMS

TIER 3 Intensive, Individual Interventions
- Individual students
- Assessment-based
- High intensity
- Of longer duration

CIRCA 5%

TIER 2 Targeted Group Interventions
- Some students (at-risk)
- High efficiency
- Rapid response

CIRCA 15%

TIER 1 Core Instructional Interventions
- All students
- Preventive, proactive

CIRCA 80%

BEHAVIORAL SYSTEMS

TIER 3 Intensive, Individual Interventions
- Individual students
- Assessment-based
- Intense, durable procedures

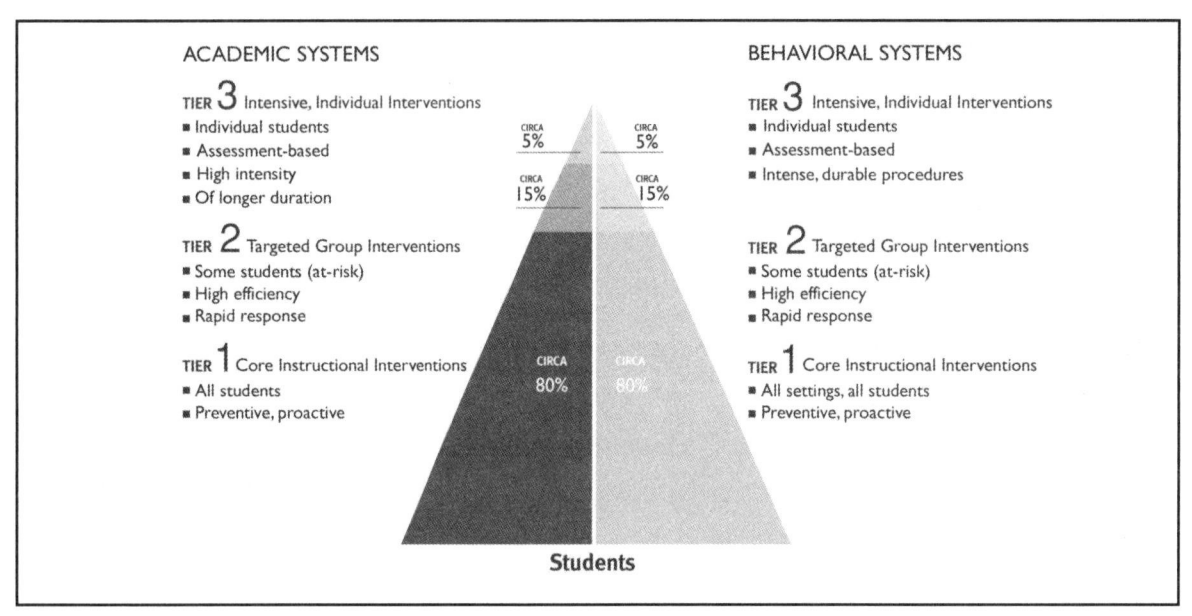

CIRCA 5%

TIER 2 Targeted Group Interventions
- Some students (at-risk)
- High efficiency
- Rapid response

CIRCA 15%

TIER 1 Core Instructional Interventions
- All settings, all students
- Preventive, proactive

CIRCA 80%

Students

Figure 3.1. Three-tier system of RtI.

Batsch, G., Elliott, J., Graden, J., Grimes, J., Kovaleski, J., Prasse, D. et al. (2006). *Response to intervention: Policy considerations and implementation.* Alexandria, VA: NASDSE. Reprinted with permission.

OCCUPATIONAL THERAPY AND COLLABORATION

An OT is a valuable resource for collaborating with educational staff when there is a concern regarding a student's performance in school. However, it can be difficult to know how, where, and when to initiate contact. The Teacher Observation Checklist on pages 26-27 is a helpful starting place (see also the reproducible copy in the Appendix).

The checklist may be completed by an educational staff member and then given to the OT to review. As needed, the OT can schedule a time to observe the student in the school environments in which she is struggling. Data collected through such observation are shared, and educational team members involved with the student meet to discuss solutions, including interventions and accommodations to the student's daily school routine. Further, follow-up occurs with regular frequency to determine if interventions are successful, or if a comprehensive special education evaluation is necessary to identify the need for more in-depth recommendations for student achievement.

If team members agree that a formal evaluation is necessary, the OT might choose from several standardized evaluation tools. The OT begins the evaluation by observing the student in the school environment, interviewing teachers, and deciding the specific areas that need to be formally assessed, which may include motor skills as well as sensory processing needs.

There are a number of standardized evaluations to choose from for addressing fine-motor skills, gross-motor skills, visual-motor skills, visual-perceptual skills, and functional performance. Examples of sensory processing assessments include the Sensory Processing Measure (SPM; Parham et al., 2007) and the Sensory Profile School Companion (Dunn, 2006). These two assessments specifically target sensory processing needs in educational environments and can be completed by school staff members who work with the students on a daily basis. For these reasons, they have been included here.

Assessment and Evaluation 25

Teacher Observation Checklist

Student Name: _____ **Date:** _____

Date of Birth: _____ **School/Grade:** _____

Teacher: _____ **Planning Period:** _____

Best time of day to observe problem: _____

Return to occupational therapist by: _____

Please check appropriate boxes.

Sensory Organization
- ☐ Runs into desks, doors, or people
- ☐ Does not know body parts (elbow, wrist, etc.)
- ☐ Has poor tolerance for touch
- ☐ Has poor tolerance for hands in paste, finger paint, or messy materials
- ☐ Does not identify right and left on self and papers
- ☐ Has not established hand preference
- ☐ Cannot cross midline of body with either hand
- ☐ Does not know directional concepts
- ☐ Moves excessively in chair
- ☐ Slumps at desk/leans on desk

Behavior
- ☐ Demonstrates inadequate attention span for age
- ☐ Demonstrates inconsistent performance level
- ☐ Demonstrates aggressive actions toward others
- ☐ Demonstrates impulsiveness
- ☐ Easily distracted by auditory or visual stimuli

Fine-Motor Skills
- ☐ Holds pencil or crayon incorrectly
- ☐ Holds scissors incorrectly
- ☐ Controls pencil with difficulty
- ☐ Controls scissors with difficulty
- ☐ Fatigues during fine-motor tasks
- ☐ Has difficulty stabilizing paper when writing
- ☐ Has difficulty manipulating paper when cutting
- ☐ Writes too slowly or too fast (circle one)

Visual Motor/Perceptual
- ☐ Does not recognize shapes and letters
- ☐ Cannot copy   O circle   + plus   ☐ square   △ triangle (please circle)
- ☐ Forms letters incorrectly
- ☐ Does not keep letters on baseline when writing
- ☐ Maintains poor spacing between words/letters
- ☐ Makes letter reversals (typical through 1st grade)
- ☐ Changes paper orientation when writing
- ☐ Has difficulty copying from far point
- ☐ Cannot organize work/desk
- ☐ Colors outside of boundary lines
- ☐ Does not stay on the line when cutting
- ☐ Cannot assemble age-appropriate puzzles independently
- ☐ Loses place on page when reading
- ☐ Holds book too close or too far away (circle one)
- ☐ Wears glasses

Functional Skills
- ☐ Unable to button, zip, snap, or tie shoes (circle all that apply)
- ☐ Needs adaptive equipment to function in classroom (list equipment)
- ☐ Has difficulty finding way to familiar places at school (cafeteria, office, bathroom)
- ☐ Does not follow directions or remember routines
- ☐ Demonstrates poor self help skills: eating, dressing, hand washing, other_____ (circle)

Attach handwriting samples if area of concern.

Comments/Concerns:_____

_____

_____

_____

_____

_____

_____

SENSORY PROCESSING MEASURE (SPM)
(Contributed by Diana A. Henry, M.S., OTR/L, FAOTA)

The Sensory Processing Measure (SPM; Parham et al., 2007) is a new way of obtaining a complete picture of children's sensory functioning across environments, including home, main classroom, art, music, P.E., recess, cafeteria, and on the bus. It provides an opportunity to compare performance between school and home, designed specifically for academic, community, and home teams. It is a standardized, norm-referenced instrument yielding scores for five sensory systems (vestibular, proprioceptive, tactile, visual, and auditory) as well as praxis (motor planning and ideation) and social participation. Supporting the principles of RtI and encouraging collaboration, the SPM helps answer the question "Is the behavior sensory driven?" It is standardized for children ages 5 through 12. For further information, please visit www.ateachabout.com.

SENSORY PROFILE SCHOOL COMPANION

The Sensory Profile School Companion (SPSC; Dunn, 2006) is an evaluation tool for gleaning information about how a student is processing sensory input in the school environment. The SPSC is a standardized 62-item questionnaire completed by a teacher regarding a student's response to sensory events in the school environment. It is divided into four areas, called School Factors (Dunn, 2007).

School Factor 1 – items reflecting a student's need for supports in the school environment. A student scoring "more than others" in this factor is sensory seeking and has poor sensory registration, indicating the need for additional sensory input for attention and engagement in learning.

School Factor 2 – items reflecting a student's attention and awareness in the classroom setting. A student scoring "more than others" in this factor is sensory seeking and sensory sensitive, indicating distractibility from irrelevant stimuli in the school environment and needs help with focusing attention to stay on task.

School Factor 3 – items reflecting a student's ability to tolerate sensory input in the surrounding school environment. A student scoring "more than others" in this factor is sensitive to and avoids non-noxious sensations in the school environment and quickly goes into sensory overload, making it difficult to work independently, listen to instruction, or cooperate with classmates. Such a student needs more structure and predictability for school success.

School Factor 4 – items reflecting a student's availability for learning. A student scoring "more than others" in this factor has poor sensory registration and avoiding patterns. Such students appear disinterested in learning and miss important details for participation.

WRITING MEASURABLE SENSORY GOALS: GOAL ATTAINMENT SCALING

It is difficult to objectively measure progress and functional outcomes for a child who has a sensory processing disorder due to the inconsistent and unpredictable way sensory processing challenges affect a child's performance, behavior, and engagement.

Goal attainment scaling (GAS; May-Benson, 2007) is a technique for evaluating the effectiveness of interventions based on the extent of achievement gained on established goals. GAS measures a wide variety of behaviors and reflects changes that are meaningful to the family and educators. Using GAS as a measurement tool increases staff cooperation and participation with interventions.

GAS scaling matches standard deviations and is based on a range of scores around a bell curve as five levels are identified.

The levels of performance are as follows:
-2 = Much less likely (<5%), almost never
-1 = Somewhat less likely (6-24%), seldom
 0 = Expected level (25%-50%-74%), sometimes
+1 = Somewhat more likely (75%-94%), often
+2 = Much more likely (>95%), almost always

Implementing GAS initially involves identifying the child's areas of need, creating benchmarks/objectives for addressing the problem areas, specifying the behaviors that will indicate improvement, and corroborating with family and school team for agreement with the appropriateness of the goal(s). Criteria for creating a functional goal include (a) addresses a child's areas of need, (b) reflects occupational performance, (c) is meaningful to the family and educators, (d) has a realistic intervention time period, (e) reflects sensory integration functions related to occupational performance, and (f) is understandable and free from jargon. GAS aligns well with individualized education program (IEP) goals and benchmarks for monitoring quarterly progress for special education students.

> **Table 3.1**
> **Sample GAS Goal for a Child with Sensory Processing Difficulties**
> - *Parent/School Concern:* Student has difficulty staying seated to complete schoolwork and homework.
> - *Current Level of Performance:* Student is out of his seat/chair greater than 75% of the time during a 10-minute time period and frequently does not complete written assignments.
> - *Intervention Period:* 9 weeks (to be measured at first quarter progress reporting time)
> - *Functional Goal:* Student will increase in-seat behavior so that he can complete written assignments both at home and school.
>   Percentage of time student will stay in his chair during 10-minute time period for written schoolwork and homework:
> -2 = 0%-24% of the time
> -1 = 25%-49% of the time
> 0 = 50%-74% of the time
> $+1$ = 75%-99% of the time
> $+2$ = 100% of the time

Chapter 3 reviewed response to intervention, collaboration, assessment, and goal writing for children in school settings. RtI is a systematic process by which teams of professionals can more accurately target student needs and pinpoint intervention strategies. An OT is a valuable member of the team and can contribute suggestions for practical adaptations and accommodations, especially in the area of sensory processing. As part of a comprehensive special education evaluation, the OT can address functional difficulties using observation and formal evaluation tools, and help ensure that measurable sensory goals are written using the GAS format to help track student progress for IEPs. Students who struggle in school with poor academic performance and behavioral difficulties benefit from the comprehensive collaboration of educational teams who strive to make a difference in the lives of each child.

Chapter 4 introduces sensorimotor activity lesson plans, which are one solution to helping children with SPD develop sensorimotor skills while integrating with peers. It also describes a variety of alternatives for weaving the activities into curricula and schedules intermittently throughout the school day.

CHAPTER 4

Integrating Activity Lesson Plans into Elementary School Environments

I have an "unlabeled" autistic student in my class who has not spoken one word, let alone made vocalizations. Before implementing the sensorimotor theme lesson plan activities from Learn to Move, Move to Learn (Brack, 2004) in the classroom, he had a low affect and seemed to be in his own world most of the time. Since starting the program (referred to as either Ready S.E.T. Go!/Learn to Move, Move to Learn), he has come out of his shell! During the Leaves theme, when he was throwing the different-colored beanbags in a basket, he said, "orange, yellow, green." This is a child who had never spoken a word in my class! He also stays excited and engaged during all the activities. He is much more vocal during the activities, and even when we are through with Ready S.E.T.

Go!, he is still very engaged and vocal. All of my students are much more engaged and excited than when we use the typical circle routine. I can pull more from the students cognitively during the activities. It's as though their little minds are awakened!

On all IEPs, I meet fine-motor, gross-motor, self-help, socialization, cognitive, and communication goals. Every one of these needs is met for each student during the activities. I do not have to second-guess myself or wonder if I am doing the correct activities to meet their needs. I love this program too because even though I am taking care of my students' individual needs, I can do this for all my students with Ready S.E.T. Go! activities! I have been singing the praises of this program from the first day I started it. I think it is wonderful!" (Mary Robbins, Teacher, Albany, GA)

This chapter provides a brief overview of the lesson plans that make up the core of this book and presents a variety of ways to incorporate the theme lesson plans into busy school schedules to enrich students' education.

The theme lesson plans are based on a developmental sensory integration process. They begin with activities that integrate the underlying sensory systems that develop before the child is born (vestibular, proprioception, tactile, visual, auditory). They proceed to activities that stimulate motor skill acquisition necessary for children to progress through developmental milestones such as running, jumping, skipping, and physical education and sport skills. Integration of the underlying sensory systems and motor skills supports language development and emotional/social development while preparing the brain for learning readiness.

The lesson plans are comprised of seven activities that relate to a specific theme and are structured as follows:

1. **Warm-Up**: Introduces the theme and may involve singing a song or reading a book.
2. **Vestibular**: Movement activity stimulates structures in the inner ear that detect changes in head position.
3. **Proprioception**: Heavy work activity, which stimulates receptors in the muscles, joints, and tendons for contraction and pressure touch. This pressure touch input organizes the nervous system in such a way that it has a positive impact on a child's attention span and emotional well-being.
4. **Balance**: Activity involves static and dynamic balance tasks such as walking on a balance beam and hopping on one foot. These balance skills help a child with functional activities such as safely walking up and down stairs,

playing on playground equipment, and navigating around objects and people in the school environment.

5. **Eye-Hand Coordination:** Activity involves basic visual motor skills such as catching and throwing.
6. **Cool-Down:** Prepares children for focusing on the fine-motor task coming next.
7. **Fine-Motor:** Activity involves using the muscles of the hands to improve dexterity for functional skills.

A theme lesson plan, when completed all at one time, generally takes about 45 to 60 minutes. In elementary school environments, teachers have tight schedules and mandatory curricula to adhere to, making it challenging to integrate entire theme lesson plans into the daily routines. There are several creative solutions to this dilemma, some of which are listed below. These solutions require effective collaboration between staff members in the school setting.

Fitting the Lesson Plans into the Daily Schedule

Each theme lesson plan involves reading a book to develop students' literacy skills. Some of the children's literature in the lesson plans may take more than a few minutes to read, making the total time for the theme lesson plan too long to complete all at once within a typical elementary school schedule.

Alternative options include reading a portion of the book to convey the main idea, paraphrasing the story in the book, reading the book earlier in the morning and completing the remainder of the theme lesson plan activities later in the day, or reading the book the day before the theme lesson plan activities and re-telling it during the Warm-Up rather than reading the book word for word.

The lesson plans may be implemented intermittently throughout the school day as a way to comply with the federal mandates of the Individuals with Disabilities Education Improvement Act of 2004 and maintain the least restrictive environment; in other words, providing services in a student's natural setting. In the remainder of this chapter, we will look at how the activities can be carried out in physical education class, as a structured recess time, center time in the general education classroom, imbedded into the curriculum, and after school as a therapeutic playgroup.

PHYSICAL EDUCATION CLASS

Begin with the warm-up activity initiated in the general education classroom a few minutes prior to P.E. class. Once the students have transitioned into the gymnasium or other room for P.E., the large-motor activities may be carried out. Thus, the students will engage in the movement/vestibular activity, then the heavy work/proprioceptive activity, next the balance activity, finishing with the eye-hand coordination activity. The physical education teacher reinforces the theme for the chosen lesson plan during the large-motor activities.

Adaptive P.E.

Implementing the theme activities during P.E. class is an excellent opportunity to integrate adaptive P.E. by providing modifications to activities and equipment for students identified as having disability-related difficulties that impact participation in P.E.

Using the Insects theme (see page 105) as an example, the classroom teacher begins the lesson plan prior to transitioning to physical education class with the warm-up activity of having the students recite the butterfly chant. The chant can be written on the chalkboard in the general education classroom so the students can read along.

Once the students are in the gymnasium, the P.E. teacher describes and demonstrates the next activity, having the students pretend they are bumble bees flying to colored spots (pretend flowers) spread around the gym. Flight patterns can vary from walking on tiptoes to walking on knees, etc. The P.E. teacher proceeds to the next activity, proprioception, and demonstrates jumping and swatting a picture of a bug (with grade-level sight words included) taped on the wall. The next activity involves an obstacle course with crawling and looking for pretend bugs using a tunnel, balance beam, hula-hoop circles, and other equipment. The final activity carried out in the gym involves the eye-hand coordination task of tossing and catching beanbag "bugs" in nets with a partner.

The cool-down could be used as a transition activity when the students arrive in the next location, whether that is music, art, or homeroom. If the students are going to lunch after P.E., the cool-down could be completed at the end of P.E. in the gymnasium. If the cool-down is reading a lengthy book and the students are not going back to their homeroom after P.E., the P.E. teacher, music teacher, art teacher, etc., could tell the storyline in the selected book, rather than reading the book cover to cover. This would be an excellent way to carry on the lost art of story-telling.

Depending on the teacher's schedule for the day, the fine-motor activity could be completed immediately after P.E. when the students return to the classroom or later in the day. If the fine-motor activity is done later in the day, the teacher simply reiterates the theme in the lesson plan prior to introducing the fine-motor activity to refresh students' memory. If the students are going to art class after P.E., the fine-motor activity is easily completed at that time.

RECESS – OUTDOOR/INDOOR

Recess is vital to a child's physical growth and social development. In some schools recess is abolished from the school day or considerably reduced for a variety of reasons, including the need for more instructional time, as a disciplinary action, or due to safety/liability issues. This is very unfortunate as research supports the connection between learning and physical activity.

Jarrett and Maxwell (2000) cite several areas where recess is important – learning, social development, and health. Research has shown that the brain requires intermittent changes and downtime for memory and attention to be optimal (Jensen, 1998). Pellegrini (1995) and Pellegrini and Davis (1993) found that elementary school children had more difficulty paying attention when recess was delayed. Further, Jarrett et al. (1998) discovered that on recess days, fourth-grade students were less fidgety and better able to stay on task.

Recess provides a break from the cognitive academic day and can help children be "brain ready" for their best possible learning. It is also an opportunity for children to interact on a social level with their peers. Recess allows children to organize their own unique games and agree upon rules they make up. In the process, they learn turn taking and how to work with teammates. In addition, important skills for solving conflicts can be learned and honed during recess time. These skills are essential for lifetime friendships, employment, etc.

Physical activity is also crucial for good health. Since childhood obesity is on the rise, it is all the more crucial that children get exercise for age-appropriate fitness. Children engage in physical activity during recess by climbing monkey bars, going down slides, and running around the playground playing tag, kickball, or other sports. Studies show that elementary children engage in physical activity during recess more than 50% of the time (Kraft, 1989).

The Merry-Go-Round Dilemma

Many city parks and playgrounds are taking out merry-go-rounds because of concerns over children's safety. This is unfortunate since riding on a merry-go-round provides rotary vestibular movement, which is important sensory "food" for a child's brain. For example, rotary movement input is essential for helping children who have underresponsive vestibular processing to attain a "just right" (Williams & Shellenberger, 1996, pp. 2-3) state of alertness in order to be more focused for learning.

If merry-go-rounds are removed, schools could consider replacing them with "safer" alternatives, such as horizontal tire swings with rotational devices, spinning monkey bars, and/or in-ground merry-go-rounds (Landscape Structures, Inc. www.playlsi.com).

Recess is generally an unstructured playtime, but incorporating some of the theme lesson plans would provide much-needed sensorimotor input for brainpower, while giving children organized opportunities to improve engagement, participation, and social skills. Some children might isolate themselves during recess and have difficulty initiating interactions. The structured activities from the lesson plans could bridge the gap for these children by providing a template from which to learn how to develop friendships. The lesson plans can be incorporated into both outdoor and indoor recess.

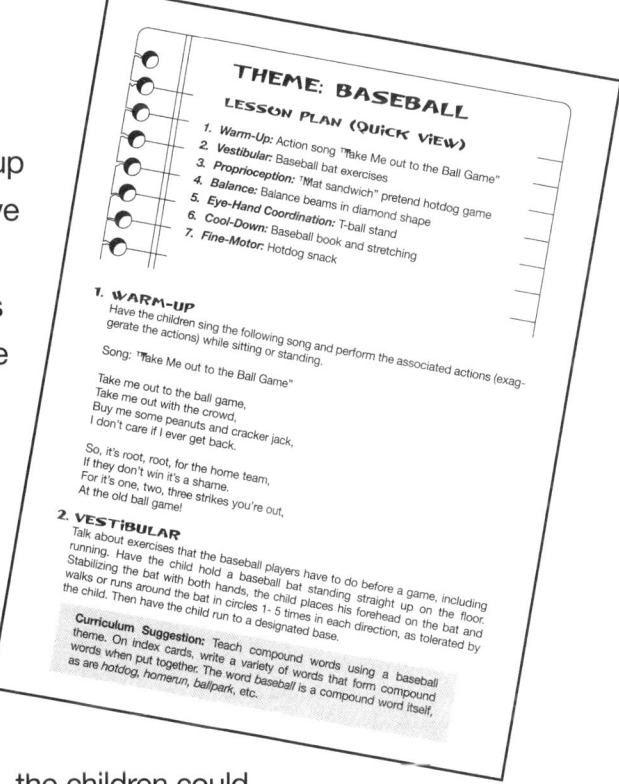

Outdoor Recess

Begin the theme lesson plan with the warm-up activity prior to recess. After the students have transitioned to the playground, have them gather as a group to be ready for instructions to the next activity. The students then engage in each activity category (vestibular, proprioception, balance, eye-hand coordination) per the lesson plan. Some activities may need to be altered to accommodate the use of the playground space.

For example, the baseball lesson plan could begin with singing the warm-up song as the children are transitioning to recess. Once outside, as an organized group, the children could perform the baseball bat exercises, the hotdog game with a mat, the baseball diamond balance task (may replace balance beams with jump ropes for ease of carrying), and finish with a T-ball game. When the children return to the classroom, they could stretch while the teacher reads a book. Fine-motor could be carried out immediately after the cool-down or later in the day. Any materials that are needed for the activities can be stored in a bin, tub, or shed near the playground, or toted outside in a wheeled cart.

Complete the cool-down activity after the students transition back to the classroom. The fine-motor activity can be completed immediately after the cool-down or later in the day, depending on the classroom schedule.

Integrating Activity Lesson Plans into Elementary School Environments

Indoor Recess

During inclement weather, recess may have to take place indoors. The theme lesson plans can easily be substituted for recess following the lesson plan as written or modified as described under Centers.

CENTERS

Since elementary classrooms typically consist of an average of 15-25 students, having the entire group engage in all of the lesson plan activities may be difficult because of the space needed and too much waiting time for turn taking. A station/center approach might work better.

Initially, the class could meet as a whole group to be introduced to the theme for the lesson and to engage in the warm-up activity together. Each of the following four activities in the lesson plan, vestibular, proprioception, balance, and eye-hand coordination, could then be divided into stations/centers arranged around the room. Students would be assigned to a "team" consisting of a small group of five or more students per group.

> *Note:* To add more creativity to the team concept and develop cooperative learning skills, student members of each team could vote on a mascot, craft a logo with team colors that could be made into a T-shirt design, or develop a fight song/chant unique to their team.

The stations/centers around the classroom could be labeled with numbers, symbols, or pictures to represent the theme and label the activity category. For example, if the theme is outer space, each station/center could have a picture of a planet posted nearby. Each station/center would have a different planet assigned to it, such as the vestibular center might have a picture of Saturn while the proprioception center might have a picture of Mars.

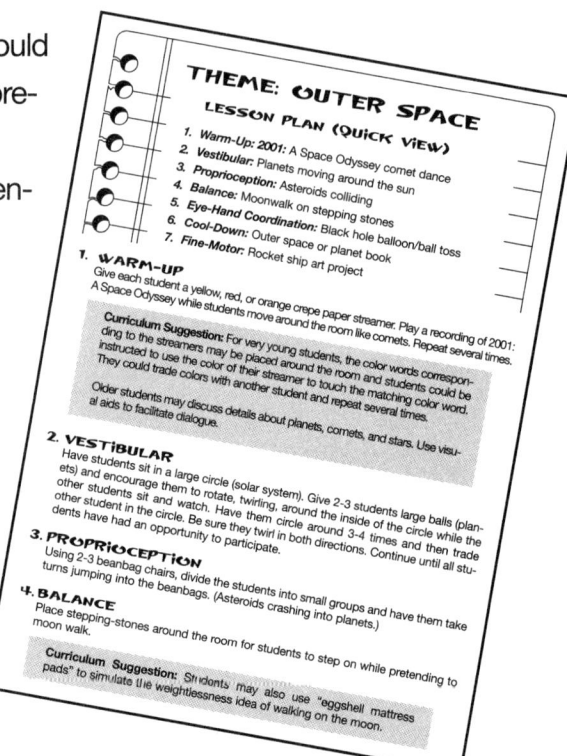

Each team would be assigned to begin at one of the four stations, stay at the assigned station for a few minutes, and then rotate to the next station when given a signal. The "signal" might be turning off the lights momentarily, briefly playing a song (refer to websites on children's music page 163), or using a cue card with a symbol that matches the theme (exp. Outer Space theme – cue card picture of planet earth).

Once the students have rotated through all four stations/centers, they gather again into one large group for the cool-down activity. The fine-motor task may be incorporated as one of the stations/centers or completed immediately after the cool-down. Alternatively, it may be completed later in the day and integrated within the context of an academic subject. For example, using the Outer Space theme, the students may engage in the fine-motor activity by constructing a rocket out of different shapes as well as constructing a diorama with eggshell mattress pieces as the moon surface and paper planets drawn around a cardboard frame. During math they can examine geometry concepts, during science they can talk about weightlessness on the moon, or during reading they can read sight words written on paper planets.

iMBEDDED iNTO CURRiCULUM
(reading, math, science, handwriting)

Creating a collaborative bridge between teachers and therapists is sometimes difficult. It is important that all school staff understand the basics of sensory and motor development and their impact on learning. At the same time, it is important that therapists understand the basics about the educational requirements students must meet to progress through the curriculum, and ultimately through grade levels. The theme lesson plans are designed to stimulate students' sensory and motor systems to physiologically prepare them for learning. If a teacher does not understand this concept, it will be very challenging to combine curriculum indicators (see below) with sensorimotor activities. This is where collaboration comes in.

> **Note:** *Curriculum indicators* are specific skills students need to accomplish at each grade level. Grade-level curriculum indicators are published by the state board of education. Curriculum indicators determine what the student needs to know and complete before the end of a certain grade level.

The activities can be imbedded into daily academic subjects through communication, ingenuity, and creative problem solving. For example, the teacher can look at the curriculum indicator for a given subject and then choose an activity from one of the lesson plans and incorporate it. For example, if a student is learning to identify numbers, the teacher could write the numbers on ping-pong balls and have the student throw the balls and run to get them and then verbally identify the number on each ball. In this activity, the student is engaged in a vestibular running task and an eye-hand coordination throwing task, and is using auditory reinforcement by saying the number out loud and visual memory when looking at the number to identify it.

Similarly, choosing the theme Outer Space, take one of the activity ideas, such as throwing beanbags into the air, and pretend they are planets. Match the science indicator – gravity, planets, physical science, "seeing things in the sky" – to correlate with state standards.

Indicators build on each other because the student needs to have prior knowledge to master the next level. Indicators may be labeled as Introduced, Developing, and Mastering from kindergarten up to second grade. Indicators that students must master by the end of second grade are prerequisite to third grade and above. As students advance through the upper grade levels, curriculum indicators focus on expansion of the foundation skills from the primary grade levels. When a student has integrated the learning indicators, he can apply them to a variety of subjects.

Example from Science Curriculum

1. Identifies *properties* of objects.
2. Classifies and arranges groups of objects by a variety of properties, one property at a time.
3. Uses appropriate materials, tools, and safety procedures to collect information.

- At the kindergarten level, students are expected to understand and have facility with #1 "identifies properties of objects."

- When the students advance to 1st grade, they are expected to have prior knowledge in order to identify an object's properties; therefore, they would advance to the next skill, #2, "classifies and arranges groups of objects by a variety of properties, one property at a time."

- Upon entering second grade, students have gained knowledge and experience identifying, classifying, and arranging objects according to their different properties. Now they are expected to be able to apply what they know in order to solve problems that require higher-level thinking about an object's properties while they create a product of some kind in class. Perhaps it would be a display for a science fair exhibit that explains how a rock of unknown origin can be classified into the correct class. Doing this would require the use of (#3 above) appropriate materials, tools, and safety procedures.

Combining several indicators from several subject areas helps reinforce learning and makes teaching subject matter easier. Daily time constraints make it necessary to integrate various content areas to be able to cover more material and make it more "real" for students. When the skills are imbedded into the content, students are engaged and more motivated to apply the skills. Being engaged inherently improves retention of skills, leading to better mastery.

For example, second-grade students researching the life cycle of reptiles might observe their class pet, which is a live-bearded dragon. In order to: 1. Discuss that organisms live only in environments in which their needs can be met; 2. Observe life cycles of different living things; 3. Observe living things in various environments; and 4. Examine the structure/parts of living things (all science curriculum indicators), the students might prepare by reading non-fiction text about reptiles, writing facts about reptiles, and creating Power Point presentations about reptiles.

Similarly, indicators for math skills include 1. Comparing and ordering whole numbers and fractions and 2. Selecting and using appropriate measurement tools and units of measure for length, weight, and temperature for a given situation. Students take daily length and weight measurements of the bearded dragon, observing him in his habitat and comparing and relating different temperatures to his behaviors. The students also figure the difference between weights and lengths, in both metric and standard units of measure. This results in practice to mastery of the skill subtraction with regrouping in math. This example illustrates how students integrate language arts and communication indicators, as well as math skills, into the science content.

Each of the sensorimotor theme lesson plans in this book provides suggestions for curriculum extensions that teachers can implement in daily academic instruction to reiterate the learning gained from the theme subject in the sensorimotor lesson plan. For example, in the Flower Garden lesson, the proprioception activity involves pretending to bury a seed in soil by having a child lie on a mat pretending to be a seed while a large beanbag chair (soil) is gently pressed on top of the child. The curriculum suggestion involves having the students engage in a science standard by describing the properties of earth materials and exploring various types of soils.

AFTER-SCHOOL THERAPEUTIC PLAYGROUPS/CLINIC SETTINGS

Using the theme lesson plans as an after-school therapeutic playgroup helps children transition more smoothly between school and home at the end of a sensory-loaded day. Therapeutic playgroup participants can be chosen and assigned to work together by grade level or ability level. Typical peer models can participate with children who have been identified as having special needs. Teachers monitoring the after-school care can organize materials needed for the activities and arrange the location where activities from the theme lesson plans can be performed. For example, the location could be in a designated classroom, the gymnasium, the cafeteria, or outside on the playground.

It is important that a therapist monitor the program to make sure that activities are carried out appropriately. Special notes can be sent home to get signed permission for children to participate in the after-school group activities. This gives parents the option of choosing whether their child will participate in the therapeutic playgroup or engage in other after-school activities offered by the school.

For therapists working in private clinic settings, the themed lesson plans may be implemented as part of a child's ongoing therapy as a group session. Group sessions could take place with any frequency that seems appropriate. (Example: 1-2 times per week for 8-12 weeks.) Therapists can advertise in their communities and invite typical peers to sign up for the group sessions. Involving typical community peers in the sessions allows the children receiving clinic occupational therapy, physical therapy, or speech therapy services to develop important social skills as they work on fine-motor, gross-motor, and speech/language skills.

TRANSITIONS

Some children with SPD struggle with accommodating to changes in routine and, therefore, have difficulty with transitions from one task to another and from one environment to another. The transition sequence listed on page 43 provides deep-pressure touch sensation and deep breathing, both of which help a child to feel calm and focused, thereby ultimately helping him adjust to changes in routines as well as transitions between activities.

Transitions

Transitions are difficult for many children with sensory processing problems because changes in routine can cause a stress response that leads to a fight, flight, or freeze reaction. To prevent this outcome, the children regroup after each activity by sitting back in a circle on their designated spots. Monitor the group's activity level and decide whether to discontinue an activity or move on to the next, depending on the behavioral response of the group as a whole. For example, if the children are engaged in a parachute activity and the noise level increases, the children may become overly excited and fail to follow simple directions. In such cases, the adult facilitator may choose to have the children sit down while holding the parachute, attempt to calm the children by talking in a whisper and moving the parachute slowly, or discontinue the activity. Also, deep breathing and firm-pressure touch are organizing and can have a modulating effect on the nervous system. That is, it can provide a calming effect for the child who is excitable, and an alerting effect on the child who is lethargic.

The children perform the following transition routine at the beginning of group time and between each activity as needed. The children imitate the teacher leader after each step.

1. Demonstrate wrapping your arms around yourself and squeezing firmly. Then say, "Give yourself a hug."
2. Next, interlock your fingers and place them on top of your head. Then say, "Push on your head."
3. Have each child hold a small feather in the palms of his or her hands. Demonstrate taking a deep breath and then gently blowing the feather so that it stays in your hands. Say, "Blow a feather; don't let it fall." (This is an excellent way to teach children diaphragmatic breathing as it gives tactile and visual feedback.)
4. Touch all of your fingers together with your thumb to form a hand puppet. Say, "Kiss your brain," then kiss the mouth of the hand puppet and touch it to the top of your head.
5. Now say, "You're so smart; you're ready to start!"

From Brack, J. P. (2004). *Learn to Move, Move to Learn Sensorimotor Early Childhood Activity Themes* (p. 22). Shawnee Mission, KS: Autism Asperger Publishing Company. Reprinted with permission.

The transition sequence can be used in a variety of ways throughout the school day. It works well at the beginning of each theme lesson plan and throughout the lesson plan as described above. In addition, the teacher may use it after changing classes, such as upon arriving to music, P.E., lunch, or back to the homeroom class, before a test to help students prepare to focus, or at the end-of-the-school-day transition to help children get ready to go home and ease that transition, too.

This chapter explored options for implementing the sensorimotor theme lesson plans into school routines, including add-ons to the lesson plans with curriculum suggestions. In Chapter 5, we will look at learning enrichments of the theme lessons such as yoga, music therapy, sign language, and more, as well as suggestions for modification of materials and methods for children with special needs.

CHAPTER 5

LEARNING ENRICHMENTS

This chapter examines a variety of therapeutic activities that can be added to the lesson plans, such as yoga to develop muscle strength and coordination, S'cool Moves (Heiberger [Wilson] & Heiniger-White, 2000) to develop bilateral coordination and ocular tracking skills, Sport Stacking with Speed Stacks® to develop eye-hand coordination and improve reaction time, music to stimulate the auditory system and improve emotional regulation and sensory modulation, and sign language to enhance communication skills. The chapter also includes suggestions for quick activities that alert the brain to help students focus (e.g., doing chair push-ups prior to seat work), suggestions for simple modifications of classroom materials (e.g., applying a pencil grip to help a student improve handwriting legibility), and accommodations for student learning (e.g., use of headphones to drown out extraneous sounds for improved concentration).

YOGA FOR KIDS

Webster's Collegiate Dictionary defines yoga as a system of exercises for attaining bodily or mental control and well-being. Yoga is the art of movement and stationary poses combined with deep breathing to achieve relaxation and focused attention.

Incorporating yoga poses into a student's daily routine can be very beneficial for preparing the brain and body for learning. Yoga provides kinesthetic, proprioceptive, vestibular, and tactile input, and the yoga poses give feedback to the muscles and joints for improved sensory and motor skills as children engage in balance, stretching, and relaxation poses with deep breathing. In addition to improving sensory processing, yoga is also valuable for improving muscle strength and postural stability, body awareness in space, transitioning between tasks, and increasing self-awareness.

What the Research Says

Behar (2005) designed a pilot program teaching yoga to parents and their children with ASD. After completing the program, the parents reported that their children were practicing on their own at home, generally felt calmer, experienced improved self-esteem, demonstrated increased communication skills, and transitioned easier between and among a variety of settings.

Yoga helps students with visualization as they use their imagination to pretend to be different animals, shapes, or objects. Many fun yoga poses can easily be integrated into the theme lesson plans: tree pose, triangle pose, plow pose, down-dog pose, bridge pose, and the fish pose, to name a few. Pictures of the poses may be enlarged into poster size for visual prompts. Teaching the students verbally and kinesthetically the steps to complete the pose will reinforce the learning process.

Two delightful children's books about yoga show pictures of yoga poses and the steps to assume the poses: *My Daddy Is a Pretzel* by Baron Baptiste (Barefoot Books, 2004) and *Babar's Yoga for Elephants* by Laurent de Brunhoff (Harry N. Abrams, 2002).

S'COOL MOVES (Contributed by Debra Em Wilson)

S'cool Moves is a program developed by a reading specialist and an occupational therapist to improve self-regulation and brain integration. The program enhances collaboration between special education services and general education programs by providing developmental movement that supports IEP goals during pullout treatment sessions and in the classroom. Teacher-friendly Focus Moves posters are placed on classroom walls to offer movement breaks that strengthen core posture, bilateral integration, vision skills, writing fluency, and sensory processing. For example, the poster Smiley Jumps encourages children to visually follow and jump in the appropriate direction where a smiley face is positioned on a line, to the right of a line, or to the left of a line.

S'cool Moves helps children learn how to self-regulate their behavior. Children are taught specific movement routines as a group. Once all the children know the routines, the teacher holds them accountable for becoming aware of when they are losing focus, having trouble calming down, or need to be more alert to learn. Students have permission to do calming, focusing, or awakening activities in their seats. They may get out of their seats at designated times to complete a Focus Moves poster.

Encouraging children to monitor their own behavior provides more time for teachers to teach important subject matter rather than spending valuable time asking children to sit up, get to work, or pay attention. Instead of telling children to focus, teachers give students tools to help them focus using Focus Moves posters, music routines during transition time, heavy work, core posture activities, and deep pressure. For example, Rolling in Reading® focus plan 1 teaches students the Dots and Squeezies for Focus task, in which they firmly press the thumb of one hand into the palm of the opposite hand for 10 counts, applying pressure to a new place on the palm with each count.

S'cool Moves activities support children's success by strengthening the physical foundation essential for behavioral control and academic excellence. For more information, visit www.schoolmoves.com

SPEED STACKS

(Contributed by Speed Stacks, Inc.)

Sport Stacking with Speed Stacks® is an exciting individual and team sport where participants of all ages and abilities stack and unstack 12 specially designed cups (Speed Stacks) in specific patterns. Stackers race against the clock for individual times, work together as doubles partners, and compete head-to-head in team relay events. Termed a "track meet for your hands," Sport Stacking promotes hand-eye coordination, ambidexterity, speed, and concentration.

Every student, regardless of age or athletic ability, can find success with Sport Stacking. This developmental activity is taught in a specific progression beginning with the basic 3-3-3 stack, moving on to the 3-6-3, and culminating with the challenging Cycle stack. Once the basic stacks are taught, a variety of activities can incorporate Sport Stacking, including many that promote fitness, coordination, agility, and teamwork. Sport Stacking gives students the opportunity to use both sides of their body and brain in individual, partner and team activities. For more information, go to www.worldsportstackingassociation.org or www.speedstacks.com

What the Research Says

Research supports the benefits of Sport Stacking for developing bilateral coordination. Dr. Melanie Hart, assistant professor of Health, Exercise and Sport Sciences at Texas Tech University, examined the electrical activity of both hemispheres of the brain while Sport Stacking using electroencephalogram (EEG) and found that Sport Stacking utilizes right and left hemispheres. Research also supports Sport Stacking for improving eye-hand coordination and reaction time. Dr. Brian Udermann, assistant professor in the Department of Exercise and Sport Science at the University of Wisconsin, and Dr. Steven Murray, chair and associate professor, Department of Human Performance and Wellness, Mesa State College Colorado, examined the effects of Sport Stacking with 24 boys and 18 girls in second grade and found significant improvements in eye-hand coordination and reaction time.

Sport Stacking with Speed Stacks can easily be incorporated into the theme lesson plans. Speed Stacks are available in a variety of colors; orange, blue, red, yellow, green, purple, pink and black are just a few examples. The colors can represent objects from the theme lesson plans and be used for various activities. For example, if the theme lesson plan is Halloween, the orange-colored Speed Stacks cups can be pretend pumpkins. The students can engage in an obstacle course with the orange cups used as cones (pumpkins) to maneuver across the room for a relay, or they can pretend to "pick pumpkins from the pumpkin patch" and stack/unstack the orange Speed Stacks.

THE INFLUENCE OF MUSIC

Music can stimulate learning and memory (Peterson & Thaut, 2007) and have a profound effect on emotions and behavior (Hendon & Bohon, 2008). People around the world connect with music. Parents emotionally connect with their newborn child by singing to her.

Calming melodies can provide soothing comfort to an anguished child. Music synthesizes all of our senses, and integrates the physical, emotional, and spiritual self. Sometimes, turning to music can be the answer to help a child calm and focus.

Rhythm is the most important aspect of music for helping a child respond. Children naturally react to rhythm as it helps them feel in sync. Rhythm helps a child focus attention, use imagination creatively, demonstrate better organization skills, and complete tasks in a timely manner.

What the Research Says
Self-Regulation

The external structures and rhythms of music can also help a child attain sensory self-regulation (Allgood, 2005). Self-regulation enables a child to advocate for himself and make sensory choices that help him to attain a "just right" (Williams & Shellenberger, 1996, pp. 2-3) alertness level for emotional and physical well-being. Rhythms with 60 beats per minute (one beat every second) from classical music such as Mozart and other composers match the rhythm of a normal heartbeat (Rauscher, Shaw, & Ky, 1995). This 60-beat-per-minute rhythm can have a sensory organizing effect by alerting a lethargic child while also calming an anxious child.

Sensory Integration

Hall and Case-Smith (2007) used Therapeutic Listening®, a protocol that combines a sound-based intervention with sensory integrative activities and a sensory diet program, with 10 children with sensory processing disorders and visual-motor delays. After 12 weeks, the children significantly improved on the Sensory Profile (Dunn, 1999), a sensory processing assessment that measures children's responses to sensory events in daily life, and parents reported improved behavior at home. Visual-motor scores also improved, especially during the Therapeutic-Listening® phase. The authors concluded that the combination of Therapeutic Listening® and a sensory diet had a positive effect on improving sensory processing and visual-motor skills in children with sensory processing disorders.

Ideally, a music therapist is an integral part of a team and can assist in choosing music and instruments to meet the goals of students with disabilities. Some of these goals might be to improve auditory or visual processing, perceptual-motor development, motor planning, and attention span. If a music therapist is not available, music can still be woven into the students' daily curriculum and included in the theme lesson plans. The theme lesson plans involve kids moving to music with marching, dancing, and imitative actions. In addition, the lesson plans include songs children can sing along with.

SIGN LANGUAGE

Using sign language as a complementary means of communication has many benefits. Some of these include improving vocabulary and reading skills because both sides of the brain are being used, which builds more connective pathways for brain development. Signing also improves language skills, facilitates communication, assists with cognitive development, and enhances social skills by helping children with language delays communicate with others. The formation of language through thinking is synthesized with movement and allows individuals to understand and relate to others by reciprocating with sign language. Since babies develop fine-motor skills before language skills, using their hands to communicate their needs can reduce temper tantrums and frustration. Sign language can also build a stronger bond between parent and child.

Sign language uses multiple sensory systems – visual input, kinesthetic, and auditory – when voice is accompanied with a sign. Teachers may utilize verbal instruction and visual demonstration, and, if sign language is included (kinesthetic), all learners will benefit from this multisensory teaching style. Using sign language improves fine-motor skills, motor planning, and visual skills, all essential foundation skills for learning.

In the "Ready SET Go!" program, which is based on the book *Learn to Move, Move to Learn* (Brack, 2004), teachers and therapists integrate sign language into the theme lesson plans. Typically, only a few simple signs are introduced at a time, allowing students to remember the signs and eventually generalize them to a variety of settings. Facilitators can give directions to the activities with verbal instruction accompanied by sign language. In addition, simple signs for the repeated words in some of the songs can be taught so that the children can "sing" with their hands and voices. For example, in the Bugs lesson plan, the warm-up song is a traditional children's song, "The Ants Go Marching." Since the word "marching" is frequently repeated in the song, the children can sign the word and imitate marching while singing.

QUICK FIXES FOR EDUCATIONAL SETTINGS

Sometimes students need a "quick fix" to help them independently participate in functional activities and maintain appropriate attention and behavior throughout the school day. A quick fix could be a simple adaptation of materials in the classroom (pencil gripper) or a sensory activity (chair push-ups) to jump-start their brains in preparation for learning.

Quick fixes are easy to implement and take little time. Critical signs and symptoms observed in school settings for children with poor sensory processing include ineffective work habits such as chewing on a pencil rather than completing written work, poor time management, difficulty completing assignments in a timely manner, poor organizational skills, and frequent distractibility and off-task behavior. Addressing these issues is imperative for students' success.

The quick fixes in Table 5.1 are just a few examples of general suggestions that can be carried out by anyone. However, consulting an occupational therapist is recommended for decision-making regarding the needs of specific students.

Table 5.1
Quick Fixes:
Sensory Activities to Alert the Brain for Learning

- Schedule movement prior to seatwork such as marching in place, rocking in a rocking chair, jumping on a mini trampoline, swinging.
- Incorporate heavy-work exercises during the school day such as chair push-ups or pull-ups, stand up/sit down several times prior to sitting, yoga, isometric exercises.
- Include movement activities into curriculum and daily routines.
- Permit students to always have recess time (refer to Chapter 4).
- Use the Transition Sequence to gain attention (refer to Chapter 4).
- Provide occasions for students to stretch.
- Give students movement "breaks" throughout the day such as passing out papers, getting up to sharpen a pencil or get a drink of water, running an errand for the teacher.
- Give students opportunities to engage in naturally occurring heavy-work activities at school: place chairs on desks at end of day, carry milk carton crate, carry library books, help P.E. teacher with heavy equipment, help push the A.V. cart, clean/wipe off desks and chalkboards.
- Have hand fidgets available (items a child can safely manipulate for attention, such as paper clips, erasers, stress ball).
- Allow gum chewing. (Research has shown [Wilkinson, Scholey, & Wesnes, 2002] that chewing gum can increase memory by as much as 35%. In addition, chewing gum can increase alertness and thus help attention to task.)

In addition to quick fixes, simple modifications of instructional materials and methods can also be very effective, such as those listed in Table 5.2.

Table 5.2
Modification of Materials and Methods

- Adjust chair height so child's feet touch floor/adjust desk height to a level of 2 inches above bent elbow. (Research shows that correct body posture is important for handwriting legibility; Rosenblum, Goldstand, & Parush, 2006.)
- Provide a pencil gripper for students with inefficient pencil grip. (Research shows that pencil grip affects handwriting legibility only when grip patterns change during a writing task [Rosenblum et al., 2006]. Consult an occupational therapist for different pencil gripper options.)
- Allow students to stand at their desks or use a music podium on which to place books.
- Have students sit on a ball chair or air-filled cushion for added movement input. Ask the students what they think the ball chair rules should be when using a ball at their desk. Sample ball chair rules may be found in the Tool Chest handbook (Henry, 2001).
- Give students a weighted lap bag to use when sitting for added proprioceptive input.
- Have beanbag chairs available in the classroom for students to sit on while reading.
- Use a weighted vest or compression vest for an individual student. (Consult an occupational therapist.)
- Let students wear a weighted backpack for naturally occurring heavy input.
- Give a mechanical pencil to students who frequently break pencil lead.
- Use a weighted wristband for added proprioceptive input to help students' fine-motor skills ("Weigh Cool Bracelet" www.abilitations.com).
- Decrease wall decorations for students who are visually distracted.
- Allow students to wear a hat or visor indoors if sensitive to fluorescent lights.

- Mount flame-retardant Cool Shades over fluorescent lights (www.integrations.com).
- Provide a slant board/bookstand for better visual view of written material and to help support the arm for writing.
- Enlarge letter font size for easier visual reference.
- Let students use a window guide for reading if they frequently lose their place on a page.
- Use adapted handwriting paper with students who have handwriting difficulty. (Consult an occupational therapist.)
- Give students a small sticky note to use as a spacer between words.
- Tape an alphabet letter strip on desk for handwriting reference.
- Post a picture schedule for students with ASD.
- Place student's desk close to and squarely facing the chalkboard.
- Have headphones or earplugs available for sound-sensitive students.
- Play classical music or white noise in the background for students who are distracted by extraneous sounds.
- Simplify language, speak at slower rate, give one direction at a time, allow longer response time, pair directions with physical and visual prompts for students with auditory processing difficulty.
- Break tasks into small steps for students to practice.
- Use pictures or a checklist to sequence students through a task.
- Give a student cinnamon, cloves, or coffee beans to smell if sensitive to scents.
- Use vanilla scent to calm and peppermint scent to alert.
- Provide non-toxic chew items such as ChewEase pencil toppers (www.integrations.com) for students who frequently put pencils in their mouths. (Consult an occupational or speech therapist for suggestions.)
- Allow students to use a straw for drinking liquids (e.g., water bottle at desk) as sucking is organizing to the nervous system.

Learning Enrichments 53

This chapter examined therapeutic interventions that can be used in the lesson plans, such as yoga, music, and sign language, as well as unique programs such as S'cool Moves and Sport Stacking with Speed Stacks®. In addition, Chapter 5 suggested simple sensory activities that can alert the brain in preparation for learning as well as modifications teachers can apply in the school environment.

Now that we have knowledge of sensory processing and its impact on daily life, we are ready to initiate the activities in the theme lesson plans of *Learn to Move, Moving Up!*

LESSON THEMES

THEME: BASEBALL
LESSON PLAN (QUICK VIEW)

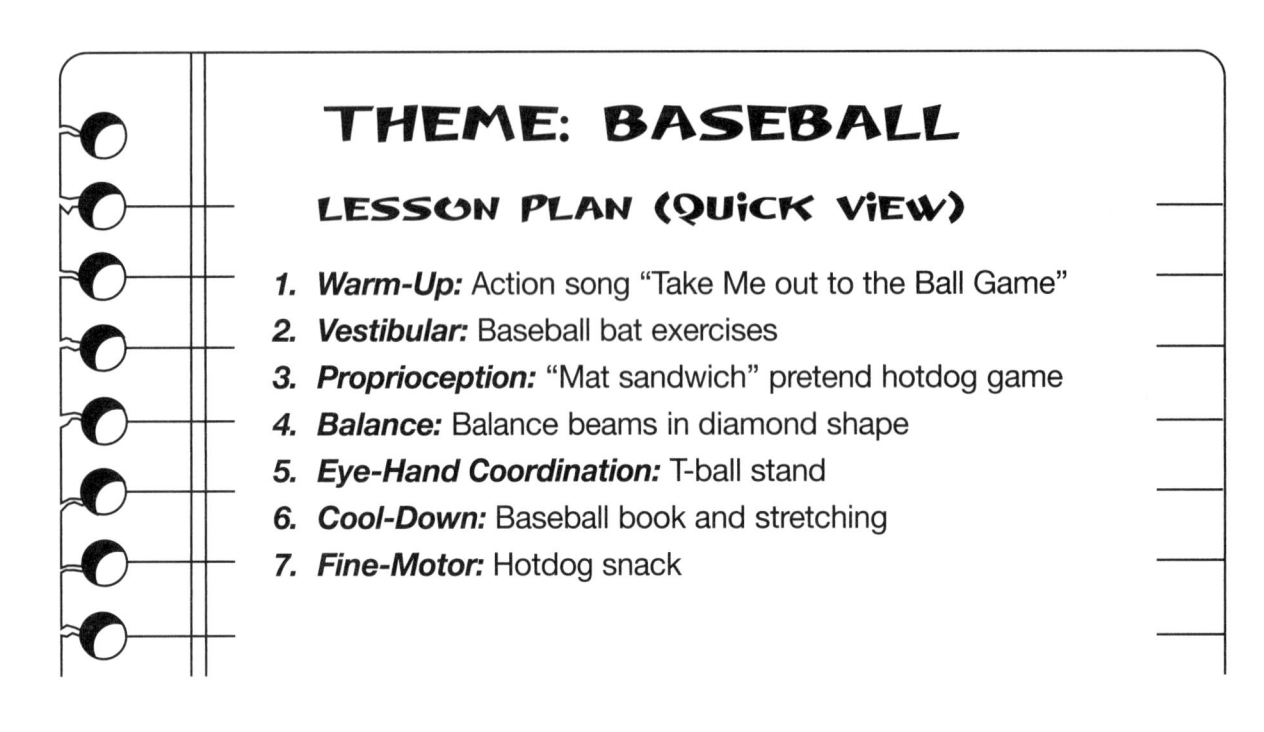

1. **Warm-Up:** Action song "Take Me out to the Ball Game"
2. **Vestibular:** Baseball bat exercises
3. **Proprioception:** "Mat sandwich" pretend hotdog game
4. **Balance:** Balance beams in diamond shape
5. **Eye-Hand Coordination:** T-ball stand
6. **Cool-Down:** Baseball book and stretching
7. **Fine-Motor:** Hotdog snack

1. WARM-UP

Have the children sing the following song and perform the associated actions (exaggerate the actions) while sitting or standing.

Song: "Take Me out to the Ball Game"

Take me out to the ball game,
Take me out with the crowd,
Buy me some peanuts and cracker jack,
I don't care if I ever get back.

So, it's root, root, root, for the home team,
If they don't win it's a shame.
For it's one, two, three strikes you're out,
At the old ball game!

2. VESTIBULAR

Talk about exercises that the baseball players have to do before a game, including running. Have the child hold a baseball bat standing straight up on the floor. Stabilizing the bat with both hands, the child places his forehead on the bat and walks or runs around the bat in circles 1- 5 times in each direction, as tolerated by the child. Then have the child run to a designated base.

> **Curriculum Suggestion:** Teach compound words using a baseball theme. On index cards, write a variety of words that form compound words when put together. The word *baseball* is a compound word itself, as are *hotdog, homerun, ballpark*, etc.

> Instructing students on how to form a compound word would be easy at this point. After placing their foreheads on the baseball bat and running in circles around it, tell students to gather word cards that you've written. Spread the cards on the floor and tell students to find as many "matches" as they can before the effects of the spinning on the bat subsides.

3. PROPRIOCEPTION
Talk about types of foods you would eat at a baseball game, including hotdogs.
Song: "Five Little Hotdogs"
(Sung to: "Five Little Monkeys")

Five Little hotdogs
Frying in a pan.
One got hot and it went BAM! (clap while shouting BAM!)

Continue the song with 4 hotdogs, 3, 2, and 1. For the last verse, sing:
No little hotdogs frying in a pan,
The pan got hot and it went BAM!

While singing this song, have the children take turns lying between two mats pretending to be hotdogs. Other children can pretend squeezing mustard and ketchup on the hotdog (use red and yellow squeeze bottles found at discount stores) and sprinkle them with onions and relish (white and green pieces of paper).

4. BALANCE
Arrange balance beams in the shape of a (baseball) diamond or make a diamond with tape on the carpet and have children walk heel toe on the beams or the line.

5. EYE-HAND COORDINATION
Place a ball on the T-ball stand and have the child stand next to it, assuming a wide-based stance as a baseball player. Have the child hold the bat with both hands and swing it to hit the ball off the stand.

6. COOL-DOWN
Have children stretch. Then read a book about baseball.
- *The Baseball Counting Book* by Barbara Barbieri McGrath; illustrated by Brian Shaw (Charlesbridge Publishing Inc., 1999)
- *The Berenstain Bears Play Ball* by Stan and Jan Berenstain (HarperCollins Publishers, 2004)

7. FINE-MOTOR
Cook hot dogs in advance. Cut hot dogs into bite-sized pieces.
Have children pick up pieces with tweezers or toothpicks, hold onto the piece while dipping into ketchup, and then eat it without dropping the piece.

Caution

Make sure pieces are small to avoid choking. Be aware of any food allergies and provide alternatives such as uncured hot dogs or vegetarian hot dogs as needed.

Materials

- Baseball bat and ball (plastic toy sets for indoor use)
- Bases (real bases if available from the gym teacher or made from heavy paper)
- T-ball set if appropriate for younger students
- 4 balance beams or tape
- Beanbags or two mats for sandwich
- Squeeze bottles for ketchup and mustard
- White and green paper pieces
- Hotdogs or wieners
- Ketchup
- Tweezers or toothpicks
- Baseball book (see book suggestions under Cool-Down)

Team: *Sakina Kapadia, Angie Kiddoo*

THEME: BIRTHDAY PARTY

LESSON PLAN (QUICK VIEW)

1. **Warm-Up:** "Happy Birthday" song with oral-motor activities
2. **Vestibular:** Musical chairs and present pass
3. **Proprioception:** Play-dough birthday cake
4. **Balance:** Piñata game
5. **Eye-Hand Coordination:** Pin the Tail on the Donkey, balloon toss
6. **Cool-Down:** Birthday party book
7. **Fine-Motor:** Cupcake decorations

1. WARM-UP

Have each child sing the "Happy Birthday" song while holding hands, seated or standing, for the start of the activity

Oral-motor activities can be incorporated following the song to increase coordinated tongue, lip, and cheek movement. The task can vary in difficulty by selecting horns of varying kinds, including horns with smaller openings/apertures, horns that require sustained cheek control and air pressure, or horns that unfurl as air is pushed through. Bubbles can also be incorporated into this activity as a way to add fun and variety.

2. VESTIBULAR

Do a musical chair activity to provide movement, auditory stimulation, and cognitive skills. This could be a pretend "cake walk" activity, in which chairs are placed in a circle (one per child), and the children walk around the circle while the music plays. Once the music stops, the children scramble to sit in a chair. Stickers of birthday symbols can be placed on each chair, while each child matches a sticker to one on a chair.

Have children race from one area to another and pass a gift-wrapped box after reaching their destination. To accommodate for children who have mobility challenges, a gift-wrapped box can also be passed from child-to-child in a variation of the "hot potato" game.

3. PROPRIOCEPTION

Give children canisters of play-dough, cookie cutters, rolling pins, and other items to make their own play-dough "birthday cake." Rolling, patting, kneading, and shaping the play-dough into a cake allows children to use their sense of touch. Various colors can be used to create detail and interest.

This activity is also highly conducive for incorporating language (verb usage) and cognitive skills. Talking about how the items feel and providing the children with new vocabulary helps to build language skills. Talking about and using words such as *long, short, big, small* (concept of opposites), and others helps to build new vocabulary skills. Action verbs can also be modeled as the children engage in the activity with words such as pat, roll, press, and others. Cognitive skills can be explored by looking at cause-effect actions as children stretch, combine, and manipulate the play-dough. For example, as colors are combined, children watch as new colors are formed or as a small piece of play-dough becomes larger as it is rolled and stretched.

> **Curriculum Suggestion:** Instruct students to write spelling words, math fact families, or practice their letters in the play-dough with a pencil or using the blunt end of a paintbrush.

4. BALANCE

Use a piñata and bat, with or without a blindfold, to encourage balance skills. Each child is instructed to strike the piñata with the bat. A blindfold can be used to challenge the child to hold the bat and strike at an item that is not seen. If a child is having difficulty swinging the bat and remaining standing, do not use a blindfold.

Once the piñata is opened, children will have the opportunity to pick up treats. Balance is utilized as children pick up treats using different motor movements of the arms and legs. Directions such as "take ___ steps forward, or back, etc." can be used to encourage following commands and cognitive skills. Clues can be given to ensure the children's success.

5. EYE-HAND COORDINATION

Play Pin the Tail on the Donkey to encourage eye-hand coordination. (Some children may prefer to play without a blindfold.) This activity can be enhanced to include a tactile element. That is, different materials can be glued onto or incorporated into the homemade tails such as satin material, corkboard, sandpaper, etc.

> **Curriculum Suggestion:** Suggest to the students that instead of playing a traditional game like Pin the Tail on the Donkey, they will play something called Pin the Prefix/Suffix on the Root Word. Play it the same way as Pin the Tail on the Donkey. Instruct students to write down any new words they do not know on a small piece of paper. Place their new words on an enlarged picture of a donkey taped to the wall. Have the children take turns spinning around and then stopping to pin a prefix or suffix to one of the root words on the donkey.
>
> **Curriculum Suggestion:** A balloon toss activity where the children toss the balloon to each other is a great opportunity for social interaction. Write math problems or spelling words in permanent marker all over the balloon and have the children solve a problem or spell a word when they catch the balloon.
>
> **Curriculum Suggestion:** Favorite birthday presents can be written on the balloons. When children catch one of the balloons, the item on the balloon can become the subject of a story they write or a sentence they write.

6. COOL-DOWN
Read a book about birthday parties.
- *If You Give a Pig a Party* by Laura Numeroff (HarperCollins Publishers, 2005)
- *The Mouse, the Cat, and Grandmother's Hat* by Nancy Willard (Little, Brown & Company, 2003)
- *I Like Birthdays ... It's the Parties I'm Not Sure About* by Laurie Renke; illustrated by Jake and Max Renke (Sensory Resources, 2005)

This is an ideal time to review all of the activities and bring closure to the themed activities.

7. FINE-MOTOR
Have the children decorate cupcakes (pre-baked and without icing or decorations) as a rewarding activity. Nonpareils, M&Ms, sprinkles, and other edible decorations may be used to explore creativity and provide an opportunity to use fine-motor skills.

> **Curriculum Suggestion:** Play the game Pick Your Birthday Gift. For younger students (K-1) or those struggling with reading and phonics skills, collect a variety of small objects in a box or bag that could be possible birthday presents – balls, specific types of cars like a jeep, etc. Show the items to the students. Have the children take turns putting their hands into the bag or box and attempt to pull out a "birthday present" that begins with a certain letter or sound. Example – You need a birthday present that begins with the /c/ sound. The child would try to find a small toy cat, a crayon, etc. It is important to show the children all the collected items and to name them prior to playing the game. This would be great practice for phonemic awareness skills in the early primary grades.

Materials:
- Party horns, noise makers
- Bubbles
- Multicolor balloons
- Rolling pins
- Play-dough
- Piñata
- Scissors, tissue, glue
- Birthday party book (see book suggestions under Cool-Down)
- Edible decorations
- Plain (undecorated) cupcakes

Team: *Shalonda N. Williams, Lesley Kranz*

THEME: BUGS

LESSON PLAN (QUICK VIEW)

1. **Warm-Up:** "The Ants Go Marching" song
2. **Vestibular:** Bug crawl
3. **Proprioception:** Stomping bugs
4. **Balance:** Beetle on his back pose
5. **Eye-Hand Coordination:** Ball of string web
6. **Cool-Down:** Bug book
7. **Fine-Motor:** Thumbprint insects
8. **Oral Motor:** Snack – ants on a log

1. WARM-UP

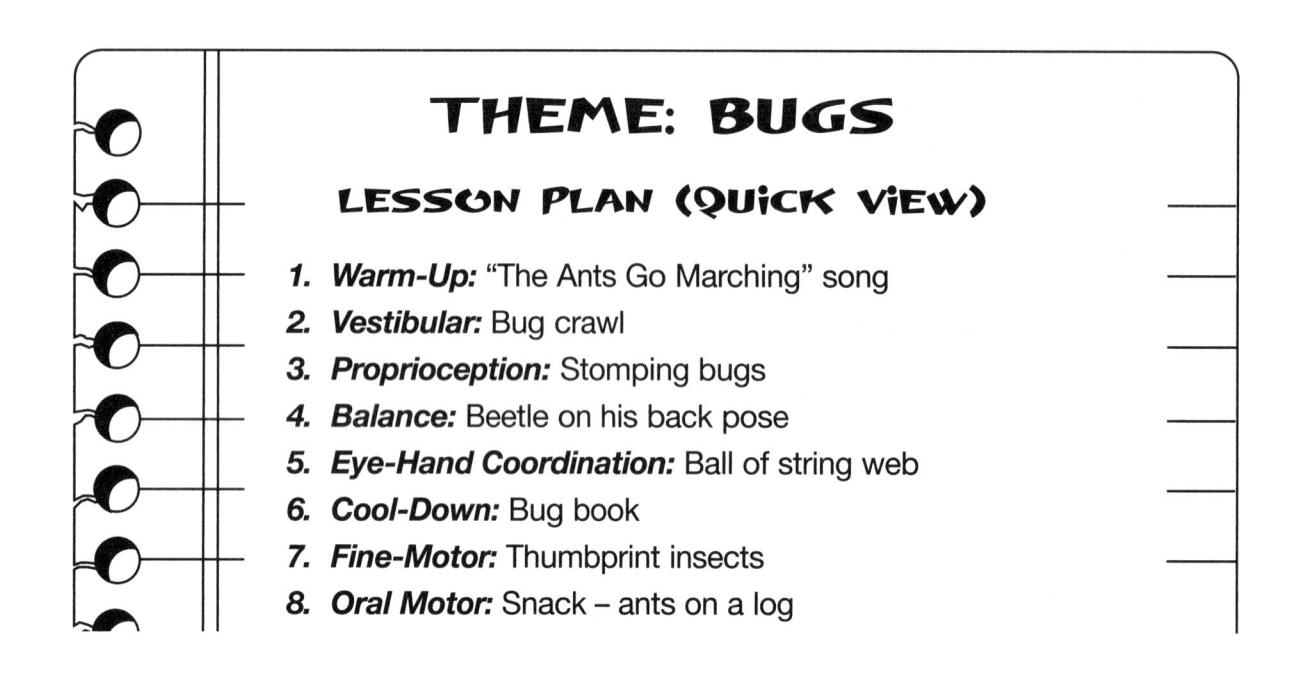

Sing the song "The Ants Go Marching"

The ants go marching one by one, hurrah, hurrah
The ants go marching one by one, hurrah, hurrah
The ants go marching one by one,
The little one stops to suck his thumb
And they all go marching down to the ground
To get out of the rain, BOOM! BOOM! BOOM!

The ants go marching two by two, hurrah, hurrah
The ants go marching two by two, hurrah, hurrah
The ants go marching two by two,
The little one stops to tie his shoe
And they all go marching down to the ground
To get out of the rain, BOOM! BOOM! BOOM!

The ants go marching three by three, hurrah, hurrah
The ants go marching three by three, hurrah, hurrah
The ants go marching three by three,
The little one stops to climb a tree
And they all go marching down to the ground
To get out of the rain, BOOM! BOOM! BOOM!

The ants go marching four by four, hurrah, hurrah
The ants go marching four by four, hurrah, hurrah
The ants go marching four by four,
The little one stops to shut the door

And they all go marching down to the ground
To get out of the rain, BOOM! BOOM! BOOM!

The ants go marching five by five, hurrah, hurrah
The ants go marching five by five, hurrah, hurrah
The ants go marching five by five,
The little one stops to take a dive
And they all go marching down to the ground
To get out of the rain, BOOM! BOOM! BOOM!

The ants go marching six by six, hurrah, hurrah
The ants go marching six by six, hurrah, hurrah
The ants go marching six by six,
The little one stops to pick up sticks
And they all go marching down to the ground
To get out of the rain, BOOM! BOOM! BOOM!

The ants go marching seven by seven, hurrah, hurrah
The ants go marching seven by seven, hurrah, hurrah
The ants go marching seven by seven,
The little one stops to pray to heaven
And they all go marching down to the ground
To get out of the rain, BOOM! BOOM! BOOM!

The ants go marching eight by eight, hurrah, hurrah
The ants go marching eight by eight, hurrah, hurrah
The ants go marching eight by eight,
The little one stops to shut the gate
And they all go marching down to the ground
To get out of the rain, BOOM! BOOM! BOOM!

The ants go marching nine by nine, hurrah, hurrah
The ants go marching nine by nine, hurrah, hurrah
The ants go marching nine by nine,
The little one stops to check the time
And they all go marching down to the ground
To get out of the rain, BOOM! BOOM! BOOM!

The ants go marching ten by ten, hurrah, hurrah
The ants go marching ten by ten, hurrah, hurrah
The ants go marching ten by ten,
The little one stops to say "THE END"
And they all go marching down to the ground
To get out of the rain, BOOM! BOOM! BOOM!

2. VESTIBULAR

Have the children get down on the floor on all fours and crawl like bugs. Scooters may be used, with the children on their stomachs crawling around collecting rubber bugs off the floor.

3. PROPRIOCEPTION

Lay out paper cutouts of bugs with beginning letters of different insects or insect words, and tape them on the floor. Have the children stomp on the paper cutouts from one end of the room to the other while music is playing. When the music stops, have each child identify the letter he or she is standing on or read the word. They could also stomp on each letter that spells out the name of a bug (e.g., s p i d e r) and say each letter out loud as they stomp and spell.

> **Curriculum Suggestion:** This is a great integration for letter or number identification. Don't forget to include instructions to stomp on multiple syllabic words the number of times to equal their syllables. Kids love doing this!! This reinforces phonics and phonemic awareness skills.

4. BALANCE

Have the children assume a "beetle on his back" pose – a yoga pose. Instruct the children to get down on the floor (use mats or rugs), lie on their backs, and grab their ankles or feet (if they can't reach that far, under their knees). Have them hold for as long as they can (1-5 minutes); they can rock back and forth, too.

5. EYE-HAND COORDINATION

Get a ball of string and pull out about 1 foot. Have the children stand in a circle. Begin with tying a loop around one child's hand and have him toss the ball of string it to someone across from him. Have that child catch it, loop a circle around her hand, and toss the ball of string to someone else, until everyone has tossed and caught the ball of string. The center of the circle should look like a web.

> **Curriculum Suggestion:** This activity is about the web idea to form a "food chain" or "web." A food chain shows how each living thing gets its food. All components of the web are dependent on one another. (Some animals eat plants, and some animals eat other animals.) A food chain always starts with plant life and ends with an animal. Most animals are part of more than one food chain and eat more than one kind of food in order to meet their food and energy requirements. These interconnected food chains form a food web. This is a higher-level science concept, but kids need to begin to develop an understanding of biological concepts as stated in K-2 science standards and benchmarks.

6. COOL-DOWN
Read one of the following stories books about bugs. Discuss the life cycle of a bug.
- *The Very Busy Spider* by Eric Carle (Penguin Young Readers Group, 1989)
- *The Very Quiet Cricket* by Eric Carle (Penguin Young Readers Group, 1997)
- *Bug Dance* by Stuart J. Murphy (HarperCollins Publishers, 2001)

7. FINE-MOTOR
Have the students make thumbprint bugs by using ink on construction paper. Draw legs, eyes, and antennas. Examples: ladybugs, spiders, and caterpillars.

8. ORAL-MOTOR EXTRA
Snack – "Ants on a Log." Provide strips of celery, carrots, or breadsticks and have the kids spread peanut butter or soft cheese on the top, then add raisins or chocolate chips. They can use their tongues to grab each "pretend bug," lick off the cheese or peanut butter, and then crunch the log.

Materials
- Mats or rugs
- Music CD or tape
- Paper bug cutouts with beginning letters or names of insects
- Bug book (see book suggestions under Cool-Down)
- Scooters (optional)
- Ball of string
- Ink
- Construction paper
- Markers or colored pencils
- Food: celery/carrots/breadsticks, peanut butter and/or soft cheese, raisins and/or chocolate chips

Team: *MaryBeth Freitas, Cheryl Wascher, Tanya Lockwood, Kimberly Miller*

THEME: CAMPING

LESSON PLAN (QUICK VIEW)

1. **Warm-Up:** "Going on a Camping Trip" action song
2. **Vestibular:** Roll the log through the forest
3. **Proprioception:** Let's Make a Tent, or Mouse in the Tent
4. **Balance:** Boat balance board
5. **Eye-hand Coordination:** Fishing off the boat
6. **Cool-Down:** Camping book
7. **Fine-Motor:** Fish card matching

1. WARM-UP

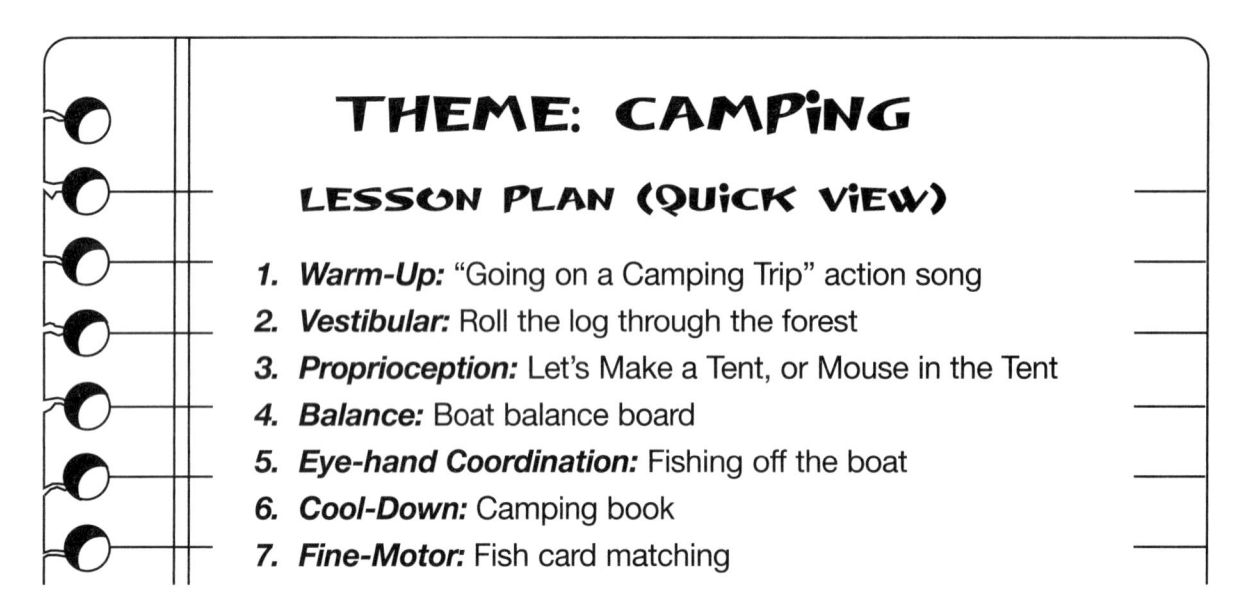

Have the children sing the following song and perform the associated actions while standing.
(Sung to: "Going on a Bear Hunt")
The children repeat each line and pat their legs with their hands in a rhythmical pattern.

Chorus: Goin' on a Camping Trip … I'm not afraid … What's that? Tall grass
    (Sweeping arm motions making swishing sounds)
    (Sing chorus)
What's that? It's a tall tree
(Arm motions climbing up, then back down)
    (Sing chorus)
What's that? Ohh, it's mud
    (March through the mud making sloshing mud sounds)
    (Sing chorus)
What's that? It's a river … We're going to have to swim
    (Swim the river)
    (Sing chorus)
What's that? Ohh it's a dark cave … I can't see anything … I can feel something
I can hear something … We better take out our flashlights
    (Take out flashlight and flick on)
Oh it's a bear! Run!

2. VESTIBULAR

Have the children roll like logs across the forest to get to the campfire. Place a mat on the floor and allow each child to take a turn to roll across the forest. Each child takes at least two turns. Have the children roll in one direction the first time and in the other direction the second time. You may have the other children sing the following song while they are waiting their turn.

(Sung to: "Row, Row, Row Your Boat")

Roll, roll, roll the log gently through the forest,
Merrily, merrily, merrily, merrily,
Life is but a dream.

3. PROPRIOCEPTION

Have the children make a tent using a parachute. Each child has to add something to the tent. They add their item by crawling under the parachute. They can add a pillow, flashlight, blankets, etc. Children can use pretend or real objects. Another option is to play Mouse. Have each child take a turn at being the mouse. The mouse crawls under the parachute and the rest of the children try to trap it.

> **Curriculum Suggestion:** Ask students to add items to the tent that can be taken on a camping trip. After reading a camping book, make a graphic organizer (simple web) that lists or shows pictures of items that are ordinarily taken on a camping trip. If technology is available to integrate, use Kidspiration software (www.kidspiration.com) to make a concept map or web with pictures/words of camping items. Have each student print them out and display on a bulletin board.

4. BALANCE

Have the children stand on the boat, which are balance boards. (Optional music can be playing while the children balance.) Time it so that each child gets approximately 30 seconds to stand on the balance board. Then, have the children complete the eye-hand coordination activity of fishing.

5. EYE-HAND COORDINATION

Have students use homemade fishing poles (dowel rod with string attached and a magnet tied to the end) to go fishing. Pictures of fish taped to juice lid tops are scattered in the water (on the floor). To work on curriculum, have sight words, spelling words, or math problems written on each "fish."

> **Curriculum Suggestion:** Make a variety of fish just as there are in real fish habitats. Choices include contractions, compound words, or different sums. Make different fishing poles that can ONLY catch certain types of fish. (Choices may be the "Contraction Pole," "Compound Word Pole," "Sums of 12, 10, 16, etc., Pole.") Students use the fishing pole to only "catch" fish that have contractions, compound words, etc. All other fish are "thrown back."

6. COOL-DOWN
Read a book about camping or fishing. A few examples are listed below.
- *Curious George Goes Camping* by Margret & H. A. Rey (Houghton Mifflin Company, 1999)
- *Fred and Ted Go Camping* by Peter Eastman (Random House Children's Books, 2005)
- *Bailey Goes Camping* by Kevin Henkes (HarperCollins Publishers, 1985)
- *Amelia Bedelia Goes Camping* by Peggy Parish (Greenwillow Books, 1985)

> **Curriculum Suggestion:** The Amelia Bedelia book may be a tool to activate prior knowledge or to introduce a lesson about the use of idioms in the English language.

7. FINE-MOTOR
Ahead of time, make different colors of fish on index cards. Draw 1-10 circles above each fish to represent air bubbles. Students can match the colored fish or the fish with the same number of bubbles. Have the students add Cheerios, for example, to create each bubble on the index card.

Materials
- Mat
- Parachute
- Tent items for props such as pillow, blankets, flashlight, etc.
- Balance boards
- Optional: music
- Fishing poles – dowel, rods, string, magnets
- Camping book (see book suggestions under Cool-Down)
- Juice can lids with pictures of fish taped to them
- Index cards with pictures of fish and bubbles on them.
- Cheerios

Team: *Melissa Daniels, Michael Daniels, Caroline Radlinger, Jennifer Konieczny*

THEME: CAR WASH

LESSON PLAN (QUICK VIEW)

1. **Warm-Up:** Action song "Riding in My Car"
2. **Vestibular:** Scooter board "car wash"
3. **Proprioception:** Bolster "car wash brushes" with spray rinse cycle
4. **Balance:** Tape "road" balance game
5. **Eye-Hand Coordination:** Paper towel toss
6. **Cool-Down:** Car wash book
7. **Fine-Motor:** Construction paper car with decorations
   Optional: Car snack

1. WARM-UP

Have the children pretend they are getting into their cars – open the door, sit down on the floor, put on their seatbelt, put the key in the ignition, and start the engine. Give each child a paper plate and have them practice steering and driving the car. "Riding in My Car," found on the Greg and Steve CD *Rockin Down the Road*, is a good song to play or sing along with for this activity.

2. VESTIBULAR

Have the children sit on the scooter. Using their paper plate to steer with, they "drive" under a hula-hoop(s) cut in half that has been stuck into two styrofoam cones. Tape crepe paper streamers onto the edge of the hula-hoop to simulate the car wash brushes. The children can follow a taped line on the floor for a "road" to drive to the car wash. Then they park the car in a parking lot with slots designated by masking tape for the next child to begin.

> **Curriculum Suggestions:** This is a perfect opportunity to instruct children in grades K-2 on how to navigate around an analog clock. Math standards and benchmarks require children to read and tell time to the hour, half-hour, and five-minute interval using analog and digital clocks. Given that students who take drivers' education classes are taught that a steering wheel should be thought of as a clock, it makes sense to teach that, too. While pretending to drive, students can use a pretend steering wheel made from a paper plate. The paper plate should be fashioned into an analog clock and spoken of as such.

When the vestibular activity is completed, be sure everyone has a "steering wheel clock." As students are sitting at their desks (which can be called the driver's seat), announce that they will be driving somewhere. Give directions for them to turn at certain points. Announce it in the same manner an adult would give directions: "Turn west on Topeka Ave, left on 3rd Street," etc. Show them how to turn the "steering wheel clock" in a hand-over-hand motion, grasping the wheel at the 10 o'clock and 2 o'clock positions whenever returning to straight driving.

Following this activity, practice cardinal directions (north, south, east, west), thereby integrating a social studies benchmark into the lesson as well.

3. PROPRIOCEPTION
Explain to the children that at the car wash, large brushes rub against the car to wash it. You may show pictures to illustrate. Use two big bolsters for the children to squeeze through by rolling on their stomachs sandwiched between the bolsters. After the car has been washed, a rinse cycle washes off the soap. Two children stand at the sides of the bolsters spraying lightly with mist.

4. BALANCE
Place a piece of tape on the floor to designate a pretend road. Have the children walk on the taped line heel to toe. Challenge them by saying that they have to drive very carefully on the road, making sure they don't make a wrong turn or drive recklessly. Otherwise, the children might get a pretend ticket from the "police officer" (the teacher or other adult), who hands out paper slips to careless drivers.

5. EYE-HAND COORDINATION
The children wipe down their pretend car with paper towels. Then they toss the paper towel into a wastebasket from a short distance.

> **Curriculum Suggestions:** Many young primary students have not mastered spatial relationship between two concrete objects using appropriate vocabulary such as *left, right, above, below, behind, on, under, clockwise,* and *counterclockwise*. Prepare a cutout of a life-sized small car on a bulletin board. Instruct students to stand in different positions around the car as you call them out.

Tell students they will be waxing a car. To simulate this and continue practicing spatial relationship directionality, use a dry-erase marker as wax. "Smear" the wax on a car drawn on a large whiteboard. Give the students a sponge and direct them to "wipe off" the wax using a clockwise or a counterclockwise motion. A similar activity would be to arrange a group of chairs in the classroom as if they were the interior of a car. Have children sit in the various chairs. Ask each student to explain to the others where he or she is sitting in the "car." They should describe positions such as *front seat, back seat, left side, right side, behind the driver,* or *in front of the passenger,* etc. Give each child a turn to be in the chair designated as the "driver's seat" until all have completed the activity.

6. COOL-DOWN

Have the children smell an air freshener. Explain that when cars get washed, sometimes a scented air freshener is used to make it smell clean.

Read a car wash theme book. Suggestions include the following:
- *The Scrubbly-Bubbly Car Wash* by Irene O'Garden (Harper Collins Publishers, 2003)
- *Five Little Monkeys Wash the Car* by Eileen Christelow (Reed Business Information, Inc., 2000)
- *Sluggers' Car Wash* by Stuart J. Murphy and Barney Slatzberg (American Library Association, 2002)

7. FINE-MOTOR

Using a simple, bold outline pattern of car on heavy construction paper, have the children color and cut the car out. For a more challenging activity, have the children trace a car template or draw their own. Then have a variety of decorating materials such as buttons, foam shapes, or pasta to glue on for wheels. The activity may be extended to make a collaborative classroom project on mural paper. The children can either drive or glue their cars on roads drawn on the paper that incorporate signs and other transportation concepts. Another idea might be having the children "drive their cars" through a paper/pencil maze worksheet, trying to stay on the road.

Extension Option: Have the children make a snack consisting of graham crackers and gummy Lifesaver candy to make an edible car.

> **Curriculum Suggestions:** To address coin identification, grouping coins, counting like and unlike coins – a difficult concept for many children in grades K-2 – have students practice in the context of a car. Explain or, if possible, model using a real car that sometimes money gets lost between the seats.

Tell students to pretend that they work at a carwash and are in charge of cleaning all the cars that come into the shop each day. One job is to search the cars' interiors for loose change. Throw a pile of large floor pillows in an area of the room. Hide several coins under some of the cushions and instruct the students to locate them, identify them, sort them, and finally count the coins they find. Kids will be getting a real-life experience while practicing an abstract skill and using their fine-motor skills to pick up and count the money.

Materials
- Music CD Greg and Steve *Rockin Down the Road*
- Scooter boards
- Two bolsters
- Hula-hoop cut in half and cones to support it. Attach crepe paper streamers (prepare ahead)
- Colored masking tape for the road and parking lot (prepare ahead)
- Paper plates for steering wheels

- Mist spray bottles with water
- Scented air freshener
- Paper towels and waste basket
- Car wash book (see suggestions under Cool-Down)
- Copies of car outline on heavy construction paper to cut out or car template
- Scissors, glue, crayons, pencils, as well as buttons, pasta, and foam pieces divided into trays
- Optional: large mural paper and/or prepared maze worksheets
- Optional: snack items of graham crackers and gummy Life Savers

Team: *Diane Bermann, Jean Imburgia, Becky Lossie, Christina Grey, Nancy LaFayette*

THEME: CATERPILLARS
LESSON PLAN (QUICK VIEW)

1. **Warm-Up:** Caterpillar book
2. **Vestibular:** Inch worm dance and/or caterpillar crawl
3. **Proprioception:** Beanbag chair sandwich (cocoon)
4. **Balance:** Out-of-the-cocoon butterfly on balance beam branch
5. **Eye-Hand Coordination:** Beanbag throw – "life cycle of a caterpillar"
6. **Cool-Down:** Flannel board caterpillar and life cycle
7. **Fine-Motor:** Caterpillar art project

1. WARM-UP
Read a book about caterpillars such as one of the following:
- *Caterpillars* by Karen Stray Nolting (Houghton Mifflin Company, 2000)
- *From Caterpillar to Butterfly* by Deborah Heiligman; illustrated by Bari Weissman (HarperCollins Publishers, 1996)

Explain how caterpillars become butterflies by discussing the life cycle of a caterpillar/butterfly. Show pictures of various butterflies such as a monarch, swallowtail, etc.

2. VESTIBULAR
Do the inchworm dance. Have the students pretend to be caterpillars. Have the children lie prone (on their stomachs) and rock back and forth on their hands, lifting their pelvis off the floor. They could also lie prone and extend arms. Tell them to bring legs forward on knees, then extend arms and repeat pattern. (These movements help develop core muscles for improved posture when seated at a desk.)

Do the caterpillar crawl. Form a row of the children and have them get down on their hands and knees. The children grasp the ankles of the child in front of them, forming a caterpillar, and move around the room.

3. PROPRIOCEPTION
Have a child lie on a beanbag chair prone on his stomach. Have another child put another beanbag chair on top of the child lying down, thereby creating a "cocoon." Explain how caterpillars go into cocoons and come out beautiful butterflies.

4. BALANCE

Have the children form a line on one side of a balance beam in preparation for walking across the beam. Before a child crosses the balance beam, have her squat down and then jump up with hands stretched high, finally walking across the balance beam like a caterpillar on a branch. Let the children repeat several times. Have them walk backwards for an added challenge. Optional: Play music in the background.

5. EYE-HAND COORDINATION

Prepare ahead of time large poster board pictures of the different stages of the life cycle of caterpillars/butterflies. Place the posters on the floor about 5 feet from a designated starting point. (Plastic circle spot markers may be used for the starting place.) Divide the children into two groups. Have them take turns standing on the spot marker and throwing beanbags onto the different poster board pictures. When the beanbag lands on a poster board, have the child tell one thing about the aspect of the life cycle represented by the poster. Let the children have at least three turns.

> **Curriculum Suggestion:** Prepare several sets of butterflies using a clothespin for the butterfly body with interchangeable paper wings. (Don't decorate the wings.) On the wings, write different math problems or single- and double-digit numbers. Instruct the students to "match" the wings to the correct butterfly by finding the one with the "sum" of the numbers on the two wings they find. Older students may be told to collect two wings, say the numbers written on them, and then add the numbers together. Program the numbers so that the students practice problems both with regrouping and without regrouping.
>
> An alternate approach would be to write different word family rhymes on the butterfly bodies and write the onsets, blends, or consonant clusters on the wings. Children can choose wings, match them up with the bodies, and see how many they can find that make real words. They can list these in a picture dictionary or other journal.

6. COOL-DOWN

Work on flannel board caterpillar. Use examples from the book *Caterpillars* to make different types of caterpillars (spiny, hairy, etc.) using pre-cut flannel pieces. Also, work on memory/recall by having students place cut-out flannel pictures of a caterpillar life cycle in order.

7. FINE-MOTOR

Give the children different-colored construction paper and ask them to cut out circles and strips. Next, have them spread glue on a large piece of paper. Form a caterpillar with the circles, having the children crinkle the legs and then glue them to the circles. They can draw different anatomical features of a caterpillar. (Teach the children the anatomical features of a caterpillar prior to the lesson plan). Make use of visual cues from the posters that are used in the Eye-Hand Coordination activity.

Curriculum Suggestion: Math standards and benchmarks require students to understand symmetry, and butterflies are perfect examples of symmetry. Explore this idea with the students and then build on their prior knowledge by introducing other objects or shapes that are symmetrical.

Additional ideas for crafts, phonics, and math available at *teachingheart.net/very hungrycaterpillar.html*

Materials

- Caterpillar book (see book suggestions under Warm-Up)
- 4 beanbag chairs
- Balance beam
- Music of choice – to play in the background
- Plastic circle spot markers (small carpet squares may also be used)
- Small beanbags for tossing
- Poster board with life cycle of caterpillar/butterfly
- Construction paper
- Glue
- Scissors
- Flannel board
- Prepare caterpillars and life cycle of a caterpillar for flannel board
- Matches

Team: *Jennifer Brown, Ashley Goggans*

THEME: CLOUDS

LESSON PLAN (QUICK VIEW)

1. **Warm-Up:** Floating scarves
2. **Vestibular:** Rolling in cotton batting
3. **Proprioception:** Passing heavy clouds
4. **Balance:** Airplane on balance beam
5. **Eye-Hand Coordination:** Cloud toss with balloons
6. **Cool-Down:** Cloud book
7. **Fine-Motor:** Paper cloud formation sequence

1. WARM-UP

Discuss weather patterns and use a science lab (see curriculum suggestion) to talk about what creates a cloud.

> **Curriculum Suggestion:** In the science curriculum for K-2, students observe changes in the weather from day to day, record weather changes daily, and discuss weather safety procedures.
>
> 1. Ask students what they see if they look at the sky. List suggestions on the board. Follow up with clouds when someone mentions it. Tell the students they will make a cloud using a 2-liter clear plastic pop bottle, matches, and warm water. (Requires teacher to light matches.)
>
> 2. Provide each student with a 2-liter clear plastic pop bottle. Have students fill their own bottle with just enough warm water to cover the bottom.
>
> 3. Light a match and let it burn for a few seconds. Each student can take a turn to blow the match out and immediately place the head of the match into the bottle. Let the smoke from the match fill the bottle. After a few seconds, the smoke will seem to disappear.
>
> 4. Have the students quickly screw the cap onto the bottle. Make sure they do not squeeze the sides before the bottle is tightly capped so none of the smoke or air escapes.
>
> 5. Have the students squeeze the sides of the bottle hard. Repeat six or seven times. Then wait a few seconds, and squeeze the bottle again, but hold the squeeze for a few seconds and quickly release the squeeze.
>
> 6. Have students look at the formation of fog in the bottle. They should see their very own cloud.

76 Learn to Move, Moving Up!

Have the children toss scarves high into the clouds and catch them while standing up. Children could also toss two scarves for "juggling." Play soft music in the background if desired.

2. VESTIBULAR

Have the children pretend they are rolling in the clouds by placing cotton batting on a mat. Have them take turns rolling forward and backward. Repeat at least twice.

3. PROPRIOCEPTION

Have the children form a circle and pass or roll various sizes and weights of balls for pretend clouds. (Heavy medicine balls provide more proprioceptive input.) Have the children name different types of clouds. Illustrate examples with pictures.

4. BALANCE

Tell the children they are going to pretend they are airplanes flying high in the sky. Have each child walk across a balance beam set up over a mat. Encourage the children to put their arms out like an airplane as they walk across the balance beam. Have the children walk forwards, backwards, and sideways, encouraging them to put their arms out like an airplane as they walk across the balance beam. The children could also squat on the balance beam to pick up cloud shapes placed on the floor alongside the balance beam and put them in buckets with the corresponding cloud shapes or cloud names.

5. EYE-HAND COORDINATION

Blow up several balloons and let the children pretend they are clouds. Divide children into pairs and have them toss their "clouds" back and forth. Using a permanent marker, draw math problems around the balloon. As the children toss the "cloud" to a friend, the child catching it can solve a math problem.

> **Curriculum Suggestion:** Replace math facts or problems with phonics blends, digraphs, or word families. Have the children catch the "clouds" and think of a word that begins the same way as the blend they touch or a word that belongs to the same word family as the one they touch.

Small balloons (water balloon-sized) may be used. On the small "clouds," write different words that have similar patterns or characteristics. Scatter the balloon "clouds" around the room. Instruct students to crawl, walk, or roll around collecting "clouds" and sorting them into categories. The categories may be boxes or containers that represent "mountains." Students must understand that clouds cannot go over the "mountains" if they are too heavy and that this is why they drop their rain first. The children would be representing the "wind" that carries the clouds over the mountains. The small balloons should be labeled with words from different word families. Example: -ar words, -ace words, -ine words, -eck words, etc. When all the "clouds" are mixed up, they look the same. Tell children they must sort them and help them over the mountain by putting them into the correct box for the family that they belong to. Repeat with different words.

Lesson Themes 77

6. COOL-DOWN

Read a book about weather/clouds such as one of the following.
- *Little Cloud* by Eric Carle (Penguin Young Readers Group, 1998)
- *Crazy About Clouds* by Rena Korb and Brandon Reibeling (Looking Glass Library, 2007)
- *What Do You See in a Cloud?* by Allan Fowler (Sagebrush Education Resources, 1996)

7. FINE-MOTOR

Have the children create a paper sequence on cloud formation. Have each child cut out the steps required for cloud formation using scissors and glue them on blue construction paper in the correct sequence. When the correct sequence is glued down, the children may use crayons, markers, or colored pencils to add details to their cloud formation sequence.

> **Curriculum Suggestion:** Have the children make a cloud in a bottle. Fill a clear plastic 2-liter bottle one third full of warm water and place the cap on. As warm water evaporates, it adds water vapor to the air inside the bottle. Squeeze and release the bottle. The squeeze represents the warming that occurs in the atmosphere. The release represents the cooling that occurs in the atmosphere. If the inside of the bottle becomes covered with condensation or water droplets, just shake the bottle to get rid of them. Take the cap off the bottle. Carefully light a match (teacher/adults only!) and hold the match near the opening of the bottle. Then drop the match in the bottle and quickly put on the cap, trapping the smoke inside. Once again, slowly squeeze the bottle hard and release. A cloud appears when you release and disappears when you squeeze.

Materials
- Scarves
- Cotton batting
- Mat
- Several heavy medicine balls
- Pictures of clouds
- Balance beam
- Paper clouds
- Balloons
- Cloud book (see suggestions under Cool-Down)
- Clear plastic 2-liter pop bottle – one for each child
- Glue
- Crayons
- Markers
- Colored pencils
- Scissors
- Blue construction paper

Team: *Nicole Stoffel, Kristi Clark, Brenda Forslund, Kate Bennett, Jorie Hannan*

THEME: DOWN ON THE FARM

LESSON PLAN (QUICK VIEW)

1. **Warm-Up:** Farm book
2. **Vestibular:** Farm animal actions with finger puppets
3. **Proprioception:** Push/pull wagons for hayride
4. **Balance:** Balance beam "bridge" over the mud
5. **Eye-Hand Coordination:** Sensory "egg toss"
6. **Cool Down:** "The Farm Song" by Skip West
7. **Fine-Motor:** Paper plate animal masks

1. WARM-UP

Read one of the book choices below (or another of your own choosing) about farm animals and review animal labels and their corresponding sounds.

- *Down on the Farm* by Merrily Kutner & Will Killenbrand (Holiday House, Inc., 2005)
- *Over on The Farm* by Christopher Gunson (Random House, UK, 2003)
- *Farm Life* by Elizabeth Spurr (Holiday House Inc., 2003)
- *The Day Jimmy's Boa Ate the Wash* by Trinka Hakes (Penguin Young Readers Group, 1992)

> **Curriculum Suggestion:** *The Day Jimmy's Boa Ate the Wash* by Trinka Hakes Noble is a good book for teaching cause and effect and story sequence. Instruct the students that they will "gather eggs" in the chicken house. Tell them that they must make it out before Jimmy's boa comes in and begins the chaos that occurred in the story.
>
> Prepare an area of the room to be the "chicken house." Set up some small containers to be the nests and fill each nest with plastic Easter eggs. Write various numbers, letters, money amounts, high-frequency words, sounds, color or number words, nouns, verbs, rhyming words, etc., on the eggs. The students must collect the eggs that you call out. For example, "Find all the eggs that include words that rhyme with "snake." Then say "Ready ... Go!" Give students 1-2 minutes to collect the eggs. Be sure each child gets a turn. Count how many and verify that they collected the correct eggs.
>
> **Note:** Eggs may be designed to cover practically any skill, lesson, or unit your students are studying.

> **Curriculum Suggestion:** Prepare cards with farm animal pictures and have students play a game of concentration using the cards. The matching cards can be number values. For example, one card has pictures of three pigs. Its corresponding card would have the number word "three" written on it. If the student doesn't get the correct match when he turns card over, her turn is over. Repeat until all cards have been collected. For older kids, increase the difficulty; for example, cards could be labeled with math problems using farm animal pictures like 6 cows + 9 cows = ? The corresponding card for this would be "15 cows."

2. VESTIBULAR

Have the children each name an animal and ask them to demonstrate a motion that they think represents the animal. After the children have demonstrated their animal's motion, have the group imitate it. Set up an obstacle course for each animal's action and have the children go through the obstacle course recalling each animal and its action (e.g., jumping over a box as if the bunny is hopping or lying down on a mat rocking back and forth like the horse does to cool off).

3. PROPRIOCEPTION

Have the children take turns selecting bales of hay that may be large or small but heavy (simulated by small and larger boxes filled with items, including books, balls, building blocks, or beanbags to vary their weight) and placing them on top of scooters or a wagon (depending on which is available). Instruct students to push or pull the scooter or wagon across the room to the coral.

If scooters are used, here is another option: Have the children select a peer in the group as their "bale of hay" and have them push the scooter with the peer sitting on it as if they are going on a "hayride."

4. BALANCE

Tell the children to pretend they are animals other than pigs and that they have to cross over the "bridge" (i.e., balance beam) without falling into the mud. If a balance beam is not available, place a line of masking tape or electrical tape approximately 6-8 inches wide on the floor with the mud (brown paper) close to it and around it. Then give students a choice of walking forward in a squatted position like a duck, on their hands and knees pretending to be a sheep, or backwards as if they were a horse backing out of its stall.

If a balance beam is not available, place blocks slightly apart on the floor positioned alternately on the left and right and have the children step towards each until they get to the other side.

5. EYE-HAND COORDINATION

Instruct and guide the children to form two lines, by gender or by counting off "1," "2" until all students have been assigned a number. Offer each child an egg such as heavy (hardboiled) versus light (empty plastic egg) or noisy (filled with beans, pebbles, or beads) vs. quiet egg (empty). If these language concepts are too advanced for the group, have them select eggs by color. Tell them the eggs are very special and that they have to get them to the farmer (the peer on the other end). Instruct them to toss the eggs by putting their arm down and slowly swinging it toward the "farmer."

> **Curriculum Suggestion:** Reinforce the concept of even and odd numbers by using the eggs as a counting tool. Before the students take the eggs to the farmer, announce that the farmer is only accepting "even" numbers of eggs at this time. The students count their eggs quickly and then send them away to the farmer. Change the vocabulary to suit your needs in the classroom. Also, be sure to use double- and triple-digit numbers for odd and/or even numbers.

6. COOL-DOWN

Have the children sing "The Farm Song." This song is available on Skip West's *Share Your Song* CD. A sample of the melody is available at www.skipwest.com.

For a group with lower language skills, you may want to incorporate picture icons. (Use cups of varying sizes pictured with each animal. As each cup is exposed, the animal it designates is the target; another option is to have the child raise her hands to label an animal without the visual prompt.)

> I went to the farm one day
> But a great wind blew it away.
> Animals, animals everywhere
> Floating through the air.
>
> Although I could not see a thing
> I could hear those animals sing.
> Animals, animals in the mist
> And the first one sang like this:
>
> (Animal noise)
>
> Now what do you think that was?
> Several children take turns guessing)
> (When correct answer has been given …)
> That was what it was!

Thanks to Skip West for permission to publish these lyrics. All rights reserved; www.skipwest.com

7. FINE-MOTOR

Offer the children a choice of which animal mask they would like to make. After they have selected one, instruct them to color it. Guide them through the craft activity as each step of the sequence is demonstrated. Depending upon the students' language level, you can add more details or steps in the sequence.

Steps: Have the children cut the pre-drawn eyes out of the plate. For children who demonstrate difficulty cutting, pre-cut the eyes. Instruct the children to pick a color for their animal (e.g., pink for pig, brown for cow) and have them color the back of the plate. Assist them in punching a hole on each side to which a string will be tied.
- Sheep – no need to color plate; glue or staple cotton balls around perimeter of the plate and add a black pom-pom for the nose.
- Cow – color plate brown; glue misshaped circular pieces of white or brown paper as the spots.
- Pig – color plate pink; offer a piece of pink felt or foam board on which they can color two black holes for the snout. A cut piece of toilet paper or paper towel roll can also be used and colored with a piece of paper glued to the front for the snout.
- Duck – color plate yellow; glue yellow feathers on the perimeter of the plate; cut and glue orange beak

Materials
- Farm book (see suggestions under Warm-Up)
- Obstacle course items (e.g., boxes, mat)
- Big and small shoe boxes or cardboard boxes to be filled
- Items used to fill boxes: books, balls, building blocks, beanbags, etc.
- Balance beam or tape on floor
- Real eggs (hardboiled) or plastic eggs with fillers such as beans, beads, or pebbles
- Wagon or scooter boards
- Picture icons of animals
- Crayons/markers
- String
- Paper plates
- Cotton balls, black pom-poms
- Pink felt, orange felt
- Glue, stapler, and scissors
- Yellow feathers

Team: *Holly Sataloff, Kate Johnson, Kelly Mosley, Michelle Castiglioni, Kelly Blandy*

THEME: FALL FUN

LESSON PLAN (QUICK VIEW)

1. **Warm-Up:** Halloween music actions
2. **Vestibular:** Spider obstacle course
3. **Proprioception:** Pumpkin bowling
4. **Balance:** Broom ride across poly beam
5. **Eye-Hand Coordination:** Toss/catch mini pumpkins/gourds with scoops
6. **Cool-Down:** Pumpkin book
7. **Fine-Motor:** Mini pumpkin decorating
   Snack (optional): Gummy worms

1. WARM-UP

While standing in a circle, have the children follow the leader by imitating the teacher's actions. Play children's Halloween music in the background. Call out actions for the children to imitate, such as gallop, skip, hop on one foot, do arm circles, touch toes (e.g., Witches Brew; www.happalmer.com; *Little Shop of Horrors* audio CD, 2004, Direct Source Special Products, Inc.).

2. VESTIBULAR

Send the students on a spider obstacle course on scooters. Ahead of time, hang black crepe paper and cotton spider webs along path by wall of the hall or classroom. Have the students ride scooter boards along the path while prone (on stomach) or sitting on scooter, using arms or legs.

> **Curriculum Suggestions:** Create paper cutout insects with numbers, words, letters, etc., written on them. Instruct students to become spiders and collect insects to "eat" as they are moving on the scooters. Modify what is written on the insects to suit/meet standards in your classroom. Example: Write words that can become a compound word when put together – *play* and *ground* may be written on two different insects. A "spider kid" could collect only words that form a new compound word. Contractions, words, prefixes, or suffixes, etc., may also be written on insects. The possibilities are endless.
>
> Explain that spiders' life cycles (Science Standard 3 for K-2) depend on other organisms in the environment.

3. PROPRIOCEPTION

Set up plastic bowling pins. Have the students roll a heavy pumpkin (with stem off) towards pins to knock them over. (Vary the weight of pumpkins, depending on the age of children.)

> **Curriculum Suggestions:** Use the same idea as in Vestibular. Write or label bowling pins with coin amounts, word family chunks, color words, shapes, or shape names. Instruct students to aim for only the words, amounts, etc., that are being studied.

4. BALANCE

Have children ride the witch broom across the poly beam (balance beam), pretending they are witches flying in the air. Have them balance pumpkins in the palms of their hands while walking across the beam. Have them step over a broomstick or pumpkins lying across the beam.

5. EYE-HAND COORDINATION

Using a real scoop (or one made out of a plastic gallon jug), have students play toss/catch with a partner or themselves with a mini pumpkin/gourd. Increase the tossing distance as students become better at the activity.

6. COOL-DOWN

Read a pumpkin book such as one of those listed below. Have each child hold a mini pumpkin. Every time the word *pumpkin* is read, have the children pass their pumpkin to the child on their right. At the end of the book, the children keep the mini pumpkin they are holding.

- *Trick or Treat Little Critter* by Gina Mayer and Mercer Mayer (Random House Children's Books, 1993)
- *Apples and Pumpkins* by Anne Rockwell (Simon & Schuster Children's Publishing, 2005)
- *Picking Apples and Pumpkins* by Amy Hutchings (Scholastic Inc., 1994)

7. FINE-MOTOR

Have the students decorate their mini pumpkins, cutting out triangles from black construction paper and gluing them on to make a face on the pumpkins. Older kids cut out their own face parts – eyes, nose mouth, ears. Cut yarn into 1-4 inch pieces and glue it on for hair or decorate face with markers.

> **Curriculum Suggestions:** Investigate different geometric shapes to address some of the math standards for geometry. For example, Standard 3 states, "The student uses geometric concepts and procedures in a variety of situations."

SNACK (OPTIONAL)
Ahead of time, string apples on a string from the ceiling. Tell students to try not to use their hands, only their mouth, to snatch the apple off the string. Have them eat the apples along with gummy worms. A drink may be served. Have students drink through a straw for oral motor input.

Materials
- Scooter boards
- Small brooms
- Poly (balance) beam
- Heavy pumpkins with stems off
- Plastic bowling pins
- Small (mini) pumpkins – 1 per child
- Pumpkin book (see suggestions under Cool-Down)
- Black construction paper and black crepe paper streamers
- Glue/scissors
- Apples – 1 per child
- String/yarn
- Gourds – 1 for every 2-4 kids
- Scoops/milk gallon scoops
- Halloween music

Team: *Kim Sleep, Shelley Stroup*

THEME: FIESTA, OR CINCO DE MAYO

LESSON PLAN (QUICK VIEW)

1. *Warm-Up:* Macarena dance
2. *Vestibular:* Piñata
3. *Proprioception:* Mexican jumping bean relay
4. *Balance:* Maraca shaking on balance beam
5. *Eye-Hand Coordination:* Matching candy beanbag toss
6. *Cool-Down:* Fiesta book
7. *Fine-Motor:* Toilet paper roll maracas

1. WARM-UP

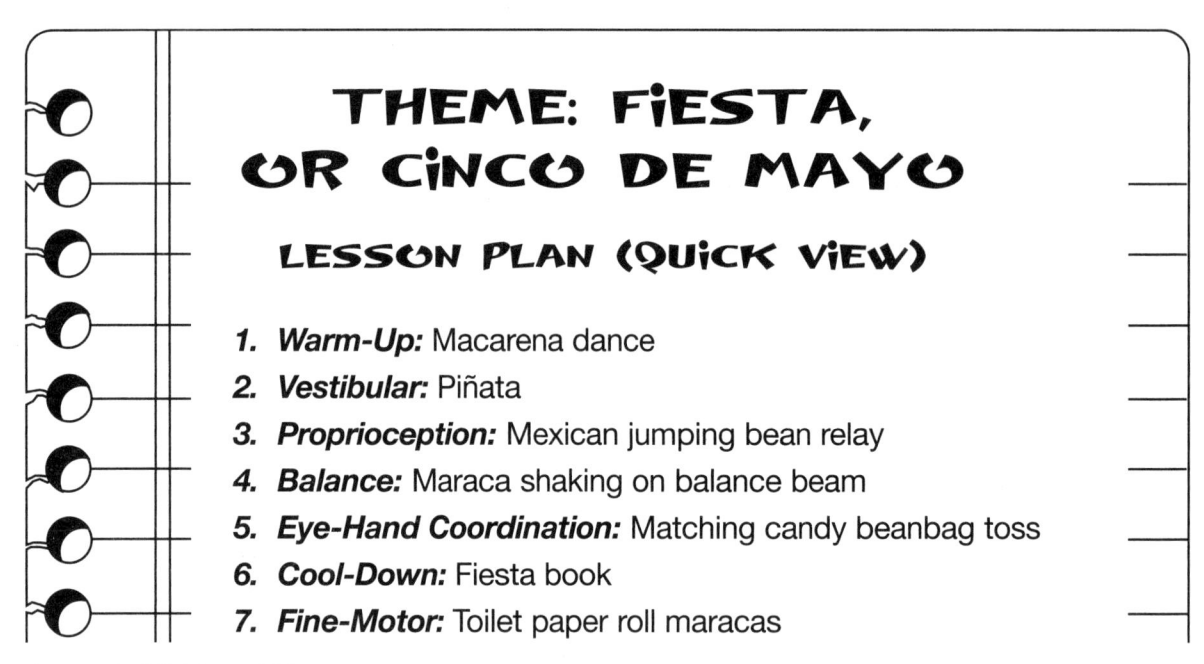

Do a modified macarena dance with macarena song (e.g., Bayside Boys). Give children the following directions: "Put both hands out palms down, and then flip to palms-up. Place each hand to opposite shoulders, then each hand on same side hip, then wiggle hips."

2. VESTIBULAR

Explain what a piñata is and how it is used. Fill the piñata with candy and have the children take turns trying to break it. While one child is hitting the piñata, the others form a circle (at a safe distance from the child who is hitting the piñata) and pretend to be holding on to a rope. They sway their arms in the air pretending they are a piñata, while encouraging their friend.

3. PROPRIOCEPTION

To do a Mexican jumping bean relay, have the children stand in lines. Each child jumps to the end of the line and around a sombrero and back again to music. Also, consider having students stand inside of an old pillowcase or potato bag while jumping. This may help them resemble a Mexican jumping bean.

> **Curriculum Suggestion:** While children are jumping, instruct them to count aloud with each jump, count in Spanish, recite math facts as they jump, etc.

4. BALANCE

Set up a low balance beam. Play music CD *Fiesta Mexican*, *La Bamba*, or mariachi music. Have the children hold small maracas in each hand and shake them while crossing the balance beam. (Shake any way up, down, and to the sides.)

> **Curriculum Suggestion:** This is a fun way to introduce new words for a word wall, spelling list, or vocabulary list. Instruct students to say the new word after you have written it on the board or the overhead. Next, tell them

to imagine that their chair or desk is a sombrero and they will use it to do the Mexican hat dance. As they move around their chair, tell them to alternate their feet in front while saying the letters to the newly introduced word; for example, to spell the word *friend*, hold arms in front of your chest with the left hand sticking up from the elbow and the right arm down in front of chest (this should look like a capital letter L in front of you). Next, switch arm positions so it looks like a backwards capital L. Hold hands in a "soft closed fist." At the same time you switch arm positions, alternate your feet in front of you. With each change, shout out the next letter of the word. After the final letter shout "olé" (oh-lay), which means hooray in Spanish. Repeat these motions three times.

5. EYE-HAND COORDINATION

On a poster board in the shape of a piñata, put pictures of candy. Place this on the floor and have children toss beanbags onto the pictures of candy. Let them name the candy they hope to have their beanbag land on prior to throwing it so that they work on accuracy.

6. COOL-DOWN

Read a book about a fiesta or Cinco de Mayo, such as one of those listed below. Have students discuss some of their own families' cultural celebrations and traditions.
- *Fiesta!* by June Behrens (Scholastic Library Publishing, 1986)
- *Cinco De Mayo* by Ann Heinrichs; illustrated by Kathleen Petelinsek (The Child's World Inc., 2006)

7. FINE-MOTOR

Make maracas with empty toilet paper roll. Staple or tape one side of roll. Fill half way with beans or rice. Staple other end. Decorate with colorful tissue paper or markers, stickers or decorative items.

Materials
- Piñata (store-bought or homemade) and plastic bat to hit it with
- Fiesta or Cinco De Mayo book (see suggestions under Cool-Down)
- Music CD: Macarena Dance, La Bamba, Mariachi Music, or Fiesta Mexican
- Poster board with pictures of candy in the form of a piñata
- Empty toilet paper rolls, beans, rice, staples, tape, glue, tissue paper, markers, stickers
- Sombrero, small maracas

Team: *Kathy Miller, Janessa Manning, Iris Hamblin*

THEME: FINDING ESCAPED ZOO ANIMALS – EQUESTRIAN THERAPY

LESSON PLAN (QUICK VIEW)

1. **Warm-Up:** Book *Hippotherapy – A Trudie Small Book Series on Children's Health Matters* by Deborah A. Tayler
2. **Vestibular:** Stuffed zoo animals capture
3. **Proprioception:** Zoo animals escape
4. **Balance:** Animals escort back to zoo
5. **Eye-Hand Coordination:** Zoo animals play
6. **Cool-Down:** Animals in cages
7. **Fine-Motor:** Drawing captured animal

Note: All activities are done on horseback.

1. WARM-UP

Read the book *Hippotherapy – A Trudie Small Book Series on Children's Health Matters* by Deborah A. Tayler (Published by Deborah A. Taylor, 2004) to get ready for the hunt.

Begin by setting the scene and telling the children to pretend they are going on a hunt for escaped zoo animals. Help the children mount their horses. Encourage the children to stretch and be ready to catch these quick animals. As you instruct them, children ride while placing their hands on their helmet, shoulders, hips, nose, knees, back, horse's mane, and horse's rump.

2. VESTIBULAR

Have the children ride around the arena looking for stuffed zoo animals. When they find one, they must stretch to capture it.

3. PROPRIOCEPTION

Some animals may not go back willingly. Have the children pretend the animal is trying to get away by stretching and placing the animals on different body parts as the instructor tells them. Example: Place your animal on the horse's rump.

4. BALANCE

The animals are happy to be with the riders. The riders can now hold them with both hands and out to one side as the instructor tells them while they are weaving in and out of upright poles and stepping around timbers on the ground.

5. EYE-HAND COORDINATION
The animals want to play with the riders so have the children place animals on their horse and the children's anatomy as instructed while changing hands with each placement.

6. COOL-DOWN
Encourage the children to pretend to go back to the zoo with all the animals. Have the children place the animals in the zoo (basket or box).

7. FINE-MOTOR
Let the children draw the animal they captured using paper and crayons/markers.

Materials
- Read the book *Hippotherapy – A Trudie Small Book Series on Children's Health Matters* by Deborah A. Tayler (Deborah A. Tayler, 2004)
- Horses and tack
- Stuffed zoo animals
- Basket or box
- 4 landscape timbers
- 5 upright poles
- Paper, crayons/markers

Team: *Cathey Ivey, Linda Hamm, Jennifer Salter*

THEME: FLOWER GARDEN

LESSON PLAN (QUICK VIEW)

1. **Warm-Up:** "Daryl the Red-Nosed Gardener" song
2. **Vestibular:** Wheelbarrow walk
3. **Proprioception:** "Bury the Seed"
4. **Balance:** Flower sway in wind
5. **Eye-Hand Coordination:** "Bugs" catch
6. **Cool-Down:** Reading a portion of the book *City Green*
7. **Fine-Motor:** Tissue paper flowers

1. WARM-UP

Have the children sing the following song and perform the associated actions. (Sung to: "Rudolph the Red Nosed Reindeer")

Daryl, the red-nosed gardener (Pretend to dig in the dirt)
Had a very sun burnt nose
And if you ever saw it, you would even say it glows.
All of the other gardeners used to laugh and call him names.
    (Point and shake index finger)
They never let poor Daryl join in any gardener games.
Then one sunny summer day, sun block came his way. (Wave both hands in the air)
"Daryl with that bright red sheen, won't you try SPF 15."
Then all the gardeners loved him, as they shouted out with glee, (Wave "Good-Bye.)
Daryl the red-nosed gardener, You'll go down in history!

> **Curriculum Suggestion:** Make this song into a Reader's Theatre so that students have a chance to practice fluent reading in front of an audience. This gives them multiple chances to read and reread the words, word cooperatively with others, and build their confidence about reading aloud.

2. VESTIBULAR

Set up cones or mark an area with tape as the garden. Have the children wheelbarrow walk to the garden area.

3. PROPRIOCEPTION

To do the "Bury the Seed" activity, have a student lie on a mat or beanbag. Then pile pillows or another beanbag chair on top of the student. (DO NOT ALLOW PILLOWS OR ANYTHING ELSE TO COVER THE FACE OR AIRWAY OF THE CHILD. ALSO, TAKE INTO CONSIDERATION CHILDREN'S TOLERANCE FOR TOUCH AND PRESSURE.) The student is the "flower seed," and the pillows or beanbags are the "dirt" on top of the seed.

Gently apply deep pressure to the student in a rhythmic pattern that gradually increases in intensity to imitate a gentle rain that becomes a more intense rainstorm. Back off as the "storm" dissipates. After the "storm" is over, the "seed" "grows" and breaks through the "dirt" of the large beanbags or pillows.

> **Curriculum Suggestion:** In science standards, students need to describe properties of earth materials, and observe, compare, and sort earth materials by size, color, and texture.

Provide an opportunity for children to explore various types of soils, including sandy soil. Ask them to describe what they feel, smell, see, and taste. They can also write their findings in their science journals. Based on the class discussion and students' prior knowledge, develop a conclusion about what soil type would be best for planting seeds. Invite discussions about this so that you can assess all individual ideas.

4. BALANCE
Ask the new "flower" (the student) to put her arms in the air and stand on one leg or on tiptoes and sway in the breeze. Try to have her balance for at least 10 seconds on each foot.

5. EYE-HAND COORDINATION
Roll multiple small balls or marbles across the floor. (These become "bugs" that want to eat the leaves of the flowers and must be caught.) Have students catch the "bugs" with an overturned plastic cup. See if they can catch them all before they roll out of the designated garden area. (This activity may also be done with students lying prone on scooter boards.)

6. COOL-DOWN
Read a book about children and gardening such as one of the following:
- *City Green* by DyAnne DiSalvo-Ryan (Harper Collins Publishers, 1994)
- *Sunflower House* by Eve Bunting (Voyager Books, 1999)

7. FINE-MOTOR
Have children make tissue paper flowers by stacking 10 sheets of tissue paper (8" x 8") together. Then fold in accordion style. Keep the paper folded and twist a pipe cleaner around the middle of the folded paper. Carefully pull each layer of paper toward the middle to make the petals of the flower.

Materials
- Beanbags or large pillows
- Mat (optional)
- Cones, tape, or rope to mark off "garden area"
- Marbles or small balls
- Plastic cups
- Gardening book (see suggestions under Cool-Down)

- Tissue paper; ten 8"x 8" sheets per student
- Pipe cleaners
- Scissors
- Optional – music and CD player to play during Eye-Hand Coordination activity "Bugs" by Rosenshotz is one option. More information is available at http://www.songsforteaching.com/rosenshontz/bugs.htm
- Optional – scooter boards

Team: *Kay Ashida, Jamie McFadden, Beth Mosbach, Rachel Boxer, Jeff Gaschler, Laura Hatler*

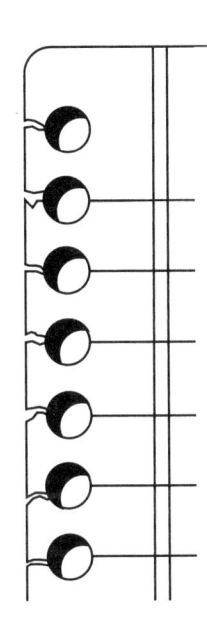

THEME: FOOTBALL

LESSON PLAN (QUICK VIEW)

1. *Warm-Up:* Football action song
2. *Vestibular:* Obstacle course
3. *Proprioception:* Pre-game exercises – stretching, bending, and crawling
4. *Balance:* Football field "yard line" tape walk
5. *Eye-Hand Coordination:* Footballs through hula-hoops
6. *Cool-Down:* Football book
7. *Fine-Motor:* Football cookie decorating

1. WARM-UP

Have the children sing the following song and perform the associated actions. (Sung to: "The Wheels on the Bus")

The coaches on the field say, "Catch that ball!"
    (Pretend to catch ball with hands to chest)
"Catch that ball!"
"Catch that ball!"
The coaches on the field say, "Catch that ball!"
On the football field.

Verse #2: The fans in the stands say, "Go, Team, Go!"
    (Raise fist into the air three times)

Verse #3: The players on the team say, "I just scored!"
    (Point thumbs back at self)

2. VESTIBULAR

Teach the children that exercise keeps your body healthy. Talk about how football players keep their bodies in shape through training exercises. Set up an obstacle course in a gym, outside, or in the classroom and have the children maneuver through the course by pushing themselves on scooter boards.

3. PROPRIOCEPTION

Tell the children that they will go through pre-game exercises just like football players do before starting a game. Lead them through stretching exercises such as head rolls, arm circles, waist bends, and lunges. Next, have them step inside hula-hoops, side to side, to simulate the tire run that football players utilize in practice.

> **Curriculum Suggestion:** Many different lessons can be addressed with a sports theme. Secure use of a digital number counter that is large enough to be seen by many kids. You'll need it to count forwards and backwards. Pretend with the children that this is the scoreboard at the football field. Program it to start at various numbers and either count up or count back. Instruct the children to count aloud with the numbers they see on the scoreboard to practice oral counting skills. This is an important benchmark skill that some kindergarten and first-grade students need additional practice to master. For older students, start the scoreboard at a higher number.

4. BALANCE

Create "yard lines" on the floor of the classroom using masking tape (do this ahead of time). Place cutout football shapes (use colors of children's favorite team) along the yard lines. Have the children take turns walking on the yard lines picking up football shapes as they try to keep their balance and stay on the line. Play music in the background, such as would be heard during a football game.

> **Curriculum Suggestion:** Before balancing on the tape, students can "kick off" some small folded paper footballs on which have been written words, letters, numerals, money amounts, etc. Do the "kickoff" as one would do when playing the game Chinese Football. "Kick" the paper footballs down the football field to make a goal. A goal can be counted by getting a football through the "goalposts" or by kicking it 30 or more yards and reading the items that are written on the paper footballs. Repeat the procedure with many other footballs and subjects from other content areas.

5. EYE-HAND COORDINATION

Have two children hold up a hula-hoop, one child on each side. The other children wait in line for their turn to throw small, soft (Nerf-like) footballs through the hoop to make touchdowns. Place a piece of tape on the floor about 5-10 feet away from the hula-hoop so the children know where to stand when throwing.

> **Curriculum Suggestion:** Suspend three different-sized hula-hoops or rings from the ceiling or by some other means. Label the rings with values from 1-3, with the largest ring being worth 1 and the smallest, 3. Allow students to "pass" three small footballs. The goal is to throw them through the rings. They will receive the number of points that correspond with each labeled ring. The children should remember how many points they get with each turn. Continue in this manner until someone reaches 20 points. Have the children keep a running total in their heads as they wait for their next turn.

6. COOL-DOWN

Read a book about football such as the ones listed below. Discuss the children's favorite NFL teams and how the players keep their bodies in good shape. If reading *If I Were a Green Bay Packer*, let the children take turns placing their own photo in the space provided at the back of the book. As the book is read, their face appears on each page through a cutout inside the Packer player's football helmet.

- *If I Were a Green Bay Packer* by Joseph C. D'Andrea (Picture Me Books, 1994)
- *Football* by Salina Yoon (Simon & Schuster Children's Publishing, 2005)
- *Football Friends* by Jean Marzollo, Dan Marzollo, Dave Marzollo (Sagebrush Education Resources, 1997)
- *Kick the Football, Charlie Brown!* by Charles M. Schultz, adapted by Judy Katschke (Simon & Schuster Children's Publishing, 2001)
- *Kick, Pass, and Run* by Leonard Kessler (HarperCollins Children's Books, 1996)

7. FINE-MOTOR

Provide football cutout cookies for each child along with a bowl of frosting in the color of a favorite team. The children use plastic knives to spread the frosting around the top of their cookies. Provide sprinkles in favorite team colors that they can pinch with their thumbs and index fingers and sprinkle on top of the frosted cookie. Provide a tube filled with black frosting so the children can squeeze their favorite football/player's number onto the frosted cookie (kids may need help squeezing the tube to write the number correctly). Provide a visual of the numbers. Let the children eat their creations.

Materials

- Scooter boards on wheels
- Orange cones and mats for obstacle course (set up ahead of time)
- 10 hula-hoops
- Masking tape to make yard lines on the floor (prepare ahead of time)
- Football book (see suggestions under Cool-Down)
- Music CD/tape to play during balance task
- 10 green and 10 gold pre-cut football shapes, or favorite team colors
- 5 small, soft "Nerf"-like footballs
- 1 cut-out cookie shaped like a football for each child
- Frosting in the color of favorite team
- 1 plastic knife for each child
- Color sprinkles in the color of favorite team
- Tube with black-colored frosting
- Small head and shoulder picture of each child
- Visual pictures of football numbers

Team: *Jodi Frailing, Paula Johnson, Bill Bahnfleth, Ginger Boldt*

THEME: FOURTH OF JULY

LESSON PLAN (QUICK VIEW)

1. **Warm-Up:** Pledge of Allegiance
2. **Vestibular:** Marching
3. **Proprioception:** Pop like a firecracker
4. **Balance:** Walk on balance beam and put stars on a flag.
5. **Eye-Hand Coordination:** Flip burgers
6. **Cool-Down:** Fourth of July book
7. **Fine-Motor:** Sparkler art

1. WARM-UP

Have the children stand and place their right hand on their heart. Recite the Pledge of Allegiance.

> **Curriculum Suggestion:** Make the Pledge into a Reader's Theatre to help students develop better reading fluency. Reading fluently is a curriculum benchmark skill in first and second grade as well as in most other grades.

2. VESTIBULAR

Have students line up. Tell them they are going to be part of a parade. Have each of them think of a pretend instrument they will play. Show pictures of different instruments (or bring in real instruments) and talk about or listen to the sound each instrument makes. Demonstrate how to march in a parade. Have children march around the classroom or hallway playing their pretend instruments. Play marching band music in the background.

3. PROPRIOCEPTION

Have students work in pairs. Give each pair a scooter board. Tell the students they are going to pop like a firecracker. Have them lie on their stomachs on the scooter board, then push off the wall with their feet. Encourage students to keep hands and feet off the ground when in motion. As the students get the idea of pushing off the wall, tell them to say, "Pop" when they launch.

4. BALANCE

Place a balance beam on the floor. Prepare star cutouts and a large starless flag. Place stars on the floor around the balance beam. As students walk across the balance beam, have them pick up a star to put on a flag. Have students place a star on the flag. Give students 2-3 turns each.

Curriculum Suggestion: On the stars, write grade-level-appropriate material for the students to pick up and match when collecting stars to place on the flag. Different "flags" could be the target for different star content. For examples, synonym/antonym pairs, capital/lowercase letters or numbers, color words, number word matches to numerals, fractions, place value amounts, nouns ONLY (or other parts of speech), math facts with sums of 10 (or any other), etc.

5. EYE-HAND COORDINATION
Tape 3-4 colored paper squares on a table to simulate a grill or frying pan. Have students flip beanbags with a spatula/hamburger flipper. Encourage students to flip the "burgers" onto the grill.

6. COOL-DOWN
Read a book about the Fourth of July such as one of the following:
- *Hooray for the Fourth of July* by Rick Brown (Sterling Publishing, 2007)
- *The Fourth of July Story* by Alice Dalgliesh (Simon & Schuster Children's Publishing, 1995)
- *Red, White and Blue: The Story of the American Flag* by John Herman (Penguin Young Readers Group, 1998)

7. FINE-MOTOR
Make sparklers by cutting strips of shiny paper and gluing them to popsicle sticks. Give each student a 9"x12" piece of shiny paper and have them cut 8" long strips, 1/2" apart, leaving an uncut area to prevent strips from separating (see below). Have them wrap the cut paper around a popsicle stick or large straw. Secure the paper in place using hot glue (adult) or tape.

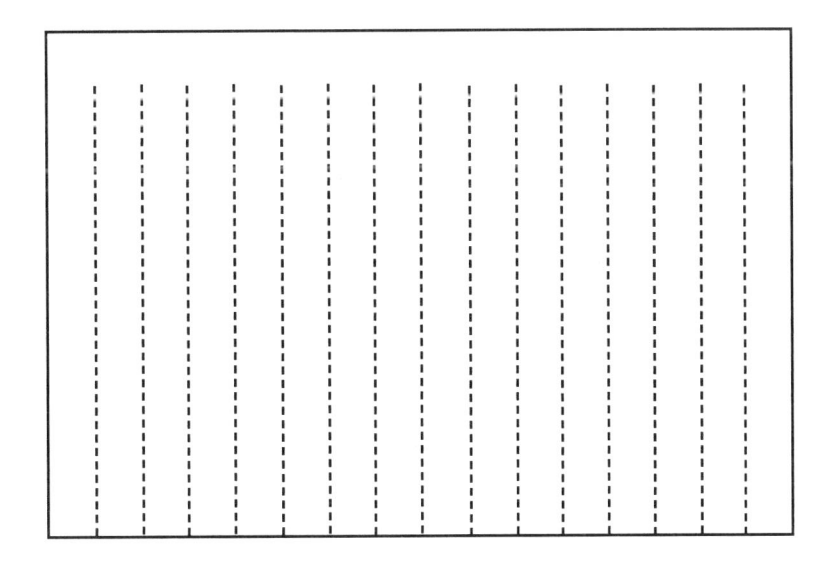

Curricular Suggestion: For younger students, math may be integrated by using non-standard measurement to make the strips of shiny paper. They could use "chain links" or "unifix cubes" to measure the appropriate length. Also, when the sparklers are finished, the students may pretend-write in the air with them. This is what kids usually do with real sparklers anyway. They could "write" spelling words, math facts, sight words, alphabet, numerals, etc. The children could also use sparklers to touch different body parts and identify them (a curricular benchmark skill for kindergarteners).

Materials
- Marching band music
- Scooter boards
- Balance beam
- Spatula
- Beanbags
- Popsicle sticks or large straws
- Shiny paper
- Cut-out stars
- One enlarged flag shape (without stars)
- Fourth of July book (see suggestions under Cool-Down)
- Tape, scissors, glue

Team: *Angie Roth, Sarah Patrickus, Maureen Mommaerts, Lisa Gross, Jennifer Cutler*

THEME: GARDEN

LESSON PLAN (QUICK VIEW)

1. **Warm-Up:** Guess the vegetable
2. **Vestibular:** Garden preparation
3. **Proprioception:** Wheelbarrow
4. **Balance:** Balance beam watering garden game
5. **Eye-Hand Coordination:** Magnetic fishing for vegetables
6. **Cool-Down:** Garden book
7. **Fine-Motor:** Seed sorting with tweezers

1. WARM-UP

Discuss and show the various vegetables (using real or plastic) that are typically found in a garden. Explain to the students that you will play a guessing game. Have 2-3 brown paper bags or shoeboxes (with a hole big enough for the students to put their hand through) each with five vegetables inside. Pass the first box/bag with the hidden vegetables. Give each student an opportunity to feel the vegetables without looking. Have students guess and then reveal the vegetables.

> **Curriculum Suggestion:** In the primary classroom, a science benchmark may be that *students discuss that organisms live only in environments in which their needs can be met*. Use this subject to activate students' prior knowledge about gardens. If any children have ever been around or seen pictures of gardens, they will know that there is soil. Some may even have had experience with digging in the soil and uncovering earthworms. Worms are a great way to get everyone wiggly. Some kids will love them, and some will be scared. Discuss earthworms as organisms that help a garden grow. Explain that the wonderful, wriggly worms will be helpful to them as they study gardens.
>
> Tell students that you will be making "word worms." Draw a crawling worm on the surface of the ground with a cut-away view of the soil below. In the soil include some plants that have sprouted above the ground line and have roots that extend into the soil below the ground line. Choose a word from your current vocabulary or spelling list and write it inside the worm. That is the key word for the activity. On each plant, write what type of word will be written on its roots. Use a different color for each category, such as "person," "thing," "related word," "synonym," or "antonym." Fill in as many words on the roots as you can think of for each category. Challenge students to see who can think of the most words that fit into the appropriate "root category."

2. VESTIBULAR

Tell the children they are going to prepare the garden for planting. Use a mat for this activity. Place foam peanuts or brown crumpled paper on the mat and have children take turns log rolling up/down the mat over the "clumps of dirt."

3. PROPRIOCEPTION

Spread out the beanbag "vegetables" in the garden. Place a hula-hoop about 10-15 feet away to represent the market. Explain to the children that we often use a wheelbarrow to get vegetables from the garden. Divide children into partners and assign one of them to be the "farmer" and the other to be the "wheelbarrow" taking the "vegetables" from the garden. Have the "wheelbarrow" get on his hands and knees. Have the "farmer" put a "vegetable" (beanbag) on his back, pick up the other child's legs at the ankles, and help him carry the vegetable to the market. When they arrive, the wheelbarrow child can go down on his hands and knees and tip forwards or sideways to dump the beanbag off. The farmer then takes the wheelbarrow back to the beginning and the pair change places.

4. BALANCE

Place six stepping-stones (purchased) and a balance beam on the floor in a line. Explain to the children that they will be walking down to the pond to collect water for the garden. Have students walk on the stepping-stones carrying an empty bucket or pail and across the balance beam. When they reach the end of the beam, have them squat down as if to fill the bucket with water (add several beanbags to bucket). Then have them stand up and walk back across the beam, over the stepping-stones, and dump water on the garden.

5. EYE-HAND COORDINATION

Place the reproducible vegetables on the floor. Give each student a card with a math problem or number on it. Have students use magnetic fishing poles to fish for the number of vegetables that equal the answer to simple math facts.

(Example: $9 \times \_\_ = 27$ or $10 - 6 = \_\_$)

6. COOL-DOWN

Read a book about gardens such as one of the following. Name the different vegetables that can be found in the garden.
- *How Groundhog's Garden Grew* by Lynne Cherry (Blue Sky Press, 2003)
- *And the Good Brown Earth* by Kathy Henderson (Candlewick Press, 2003)

7. FINE-MOTOR

Have all children identify the seeds to be used. Give each student a small cup of mixed-up seeds. Using a strawberry picker or tweezers, students sort the seeds into separate cups/plastic bags. This may be a timed event to see who the fastest seed sorter is.

Materials

- 2-3 brown paper bags or shoeboxes with hole
- 10-15 plastic or real vegetables
- Mat
- Foam packing peanuts or brown paper to crumple up
- Beanbags
- Hula-hoop or rug square
- Stepping-stones
- Balance beam
- Bucket or water pail
- 3-4 hand-made fishing poles. Attach a string to a wooden dowel and tie a magnet to the end of the string
- Reproducible paper vegetables with paper clip attached
- Cards with simple math problems on them, enough for each student
- Garden book (see suggestions under Cool-Down)
- Strawberry pickers or tweezers
- Three or four types of seeds (pumpkin, watermelon, beans, corn)
- Small paper cups or plastic bags

Team: *Jean O'Flahrity, Sonja Bagley*

THEME: HALLOWEEN
LESSON PLAN (QUICK VIEW)

1. **Warm-Up:** "We're Not Afraid" action song
2. **Vestibular:** Pumpkin patch obstacle course
3. **Proprioception:** Roll and carry pumpkin
4. **Balance:** Haunted bridge balance beam walk
5. **Eye-Hand Coordination:** Candy/beanbag toss
6. **Cool-Down:** Halloween book
7. **Fine-Motor:** Spider cupcakes

1. WARM-UP

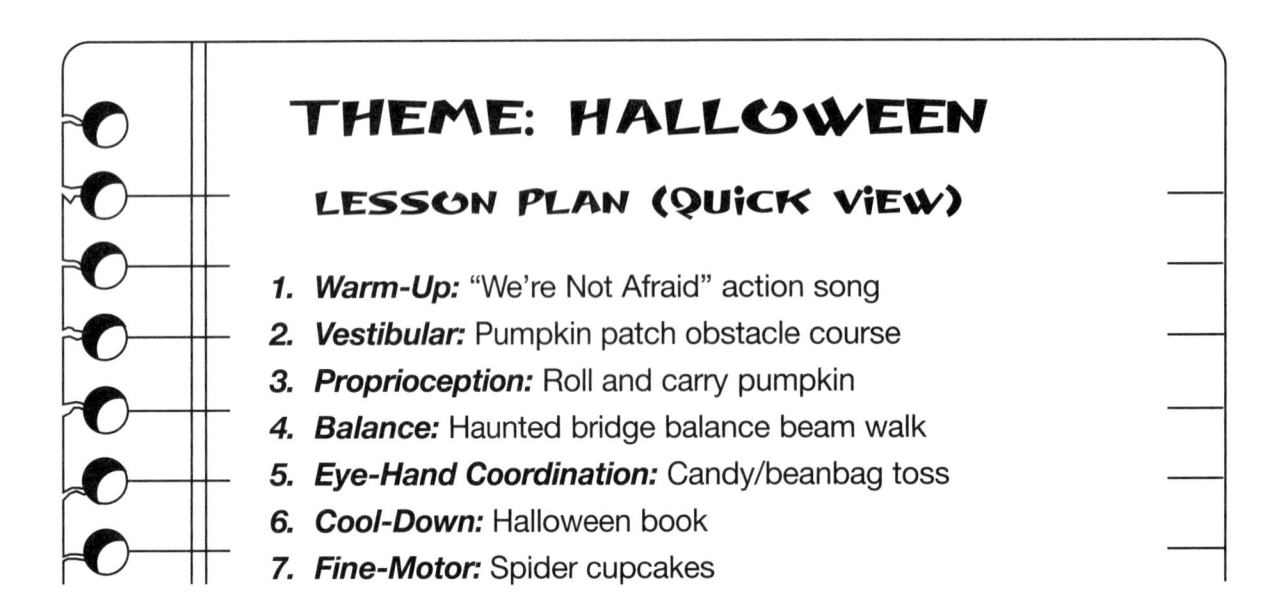

While seated, have the children sing the song "We're Not Afraid" and act out the associated movements (wiggle like a ghost, make scary hands like goblins, make cat ears [by placing their index fingers on top of their heads], and flap wings like bats).

"We're Not Afraid"
(Sung to: "Twinkle, Twinkle Little Star")
Lyrics may be retrieved from: http://www.ecewebguide.com/halloweensongs.html

2. VESTIBULAR

Have the children find their way through a pumpkin patch to Charlie Brown's great pumpkin. Set up an obstacle course using large paper pumpkin cutouts taped to the floor. Place a beanbag chair at one end of the obstacle course to represent the great pumpkin. Have the children hop, crawl, or skip through the obstacle course, ending with jumping and landing on the beanbag chair.

3. PROPRIOCEPTION

Tell the children they are going to roll a pumpkin through a pumpkin patch. To prepare for this activity, use the obstacle course set up in the vestibular activity. Taking turns, have each child roll a real pumpkin (or weighted ball) through the patch, avoiding the paper cutouts. Next, have each child carry the pumpkin out of the patch, again avoiding the paper cutouts.

4. BALANCE

Create a haunted bridge using a balance beam. Set up the balance beam ahead of time and place a large white bag (trash bag decorated like a ghost or commercial ghost leaf bag) at the far end of the beam. Have the children walk across the bridge carrying crumpled newspaper/tissue paper to "stuff" the ghost. Repeat until the bag is full. Tie off the bag and use as a decoration.

5. EYE-HAND COORDINATION

Decorate several mop buckets as jack-o-lanterns. Have the children toss candy sacks or beanbags into the buckets to "feed" the jack-o-lanterns.

> **Curriculum Suggestions:** Label the jack-o-lanterns with the words *even* or *odd*. Label the beanbags with various numbers. While feeding the jack-o-lanterns, instruct students to only feed the jack-o-lanterns labeled with the correct food (odd- or even-numbered beanbags).

6. COOL-DOWN

Read a book about Halloween such as one of the following. Discuss Halloween safety with the students.
- *It's the Great Pumpkin, Charlie Brown* by Charles M. Schulz (Perseus Publishing, 2004)
- *The Hallo-Wiener* by Dav Pilkey (The Blue Sky Press, 1995)
- *Inside a House That Is Haunted* by Alyssa Satin Capucilli; illustrated by Tedd Arnold (Scholastic Inc. Cartwheel Books, 1998)

7. FINE-MOTOR

Create a cupcake spider using prepared chocolate cupcakes, chocolate icing, pretzels, and mini M&Ms. Have the children ice the cupcakes to represent the spider body, using plastic utensils. Insert eight pretzels into the spider body to represent the legs. Place the mini M&Ms onto the cupcake to create the eyes.

Note: Make sure to check each child's food allergies prior to completing this activity.

> **Curriculum Suggestions:** Investigate math concepts with the individual pumpkins or one large class pumpkin. Instruct students to predict the number of seeds inside their pumpkin or the class pumpkins. They can write these on a chart. Make a classwide chart and graph with these data. Have students study the graph and data and answer questions about the information.
>
> Open the pumpkin. Allow the children to see, smell, and touch the insides of the pumpkin. Scoop out the seeds. Group the students into pairs and allow them to count the seeds. Explain and practice counting by twos, fives, tens, etc. Provide small paper cups for students to collect their seeds in. As a class, model skip counting by tens. This is a math counting and number sense activity that can be integrated well with this lesson. Fine-motor skills come into use easily as students pick up and count the seeds.

Materials
- Beanbag chair
- Pumpkins or weighted balls
- Paper pumpkin cut-outs
- Balance beam
- Newspaper
- White trash bag or commercial ghost leaf bag
- Beanbags or candy bags
- Mop buckets
- Triangles made of black construction paper
- Halloween book (see suggestions under Cool-Down)
- Chocolate cupcakes
- Chocolate icing
- Pretzels
- Mini M&Ms
- Pumpkin for class activity

Team: *Denise Wise, Linda Yates, Kori Vargas, Candi Adcock, Alan Amundson, Jennifer Harris*

THEME: INSECTS

LESSON PLAN (QUICK VIEW)

1. **Warm-Up:** Caterpillar chant
2. **Vestibular:** Bumblebee flying game
3. **Proprioception:** Jump and swat bugs on the wall
4. **Balance:** Bug hunt obstacle course
5. **Eye-Hand Coordination:** Bug catching with "net"
6. **Cool-Down:** Insect/caterpillar book
7. **Fine-Motor:** Caterpillar art project

1. WARM-UP

Using sentence strips and a pocket chart, write the following chant on sentence strips for the students to read aloud. This may be spoken in a "wrap" style.

Caterpillar Chant (*Author unknown*)

A caterpillar looks so small.
It is hardly there at all.
It munches on green leafy treats,
And gets bigger when it eats.
It eats and eats, till pretty soon,
It wraps up tight in a cocoon.
When it wakes up it blinks its eyes
And say, "I'm now a butterfly!"

> **Curriculum Suggestion:** Several science benchmarks and indicators can be addressed here. Begin by studying the insect life cycle. The adult insect bodies are made of three main parts: head, thorax, and abdomen. Students can "become" an insect body part simply by picking a card that is labeled with the body part name or picture. Students can crawl around the room to find two people who have different body part cards than them. Once three "body parts" have connected, they can form into an insect body by arranging themselves into the correct order: head thorax, abdomen. They must identify which is the front, middle, and rear.
>
> When complete, instruct them to make up a name for the insect they have become. Next, they can draw and label the parts of that insect, including any other parts they have learned about: eyes, antennae, six-jointed legs, wings, etc.

2. VESTIBULAR

Have the children pretend that they are bees with their wings (arms) spread out (arms straight to the side). While they are flying, they can make a buzzing noise. Have colored 10" paper circle spots scattered randomly on the floor as pretend flowers. The children are to choose a flower to start on and then "fly" to the next one.

Choices of flight patterns: spinning, up on toes, walking in a squatting position, walking on knees, really fast, really slowly.

> **Curriculum Suggestion:** Put sight words on the paper flowers. This is a great way to integrate a reading benchmark. For older primary students (later second grade), the words may be changed to study synonyms or antonyms. Give the students a word card. Students may be instructed to ONLY "land" on or "collect" words that mean the same or close to the same thing as their word card. This makes it a vocabulary lesson, too.
>
> A math benchmark may be addressed by giving the children a number; 10, for example. Label the flowers with numbers. Tell the "bumblebees" that they must collect the addends (flowers) that equal the sum that they are carrying.

3. PROPRIOCEPTION

Tape pictures of bugs with grade-level spelling or sight words at varying heights on the wall or chalkboard. Have the children jump up to swat the bugs/words with a fly swatter.

4. BALANCE

Create an obstacle course with the theme searching for bugs. Have the children carry a magnifying glass to "look" for the bugs. The obstacle course includes crawling over an object, under an object, through a tunnel, across a balance beam, and jumping/ hopping in and out of hoops lying flat on the ground. This activity is ideally done outside with shoes and socks off, but may also be done inside without shoes.

5. EYE-HAND COORDINATION

Have the children hold a net with a handle. Throw a beanbag "bug" to the children, who attempt to catch it with their net. Another option is to make the children throwers/tossers of the bugs, who then try to toss them underhand into a "net" target.

Optional Eye-Hand Coordination Activity:
Have the children hold a fly swatter and attempt to swat at bugs, which are balloons tossed into the air. The goal is to keep the bugs flying in the air.

6. COOL-DOWN

Read a book about insects/caterpillars such as one of the following:
- *Charlie the Caterpillar* by Dom DeLuise (Simon & Schuster Children's Publishing, 1993)
- *How to Hide a Butterfly & Other Insects* by Ruth Heller (Penguin Young Readers Group, 1992)

> **Curriculum Suggestion:** After reading the book *How to Hide a Butterfly & Other Insects* by Ruth Heller, which illustrates camouflage as a survival strategy for insects, instruct children to search for an area in the classroom or outside where they can blend in and "hide" like a camouflaged insect. Play a game where one or two children leave the room; they are the "predators" while the rest of the students are insects that hide in the classroom. Allow the students 1 minute to hide; then let the predators come in. Practice several times.
>
> Provide the students with different-colored coats or old clothes that they can wrap around themselves. By doing this, they experience some deeper thinking as they try to figure out the best color to suit an environment in which to hide. Finally, the whole class can discuss the significance of an insect's colors.

7. FINE-MOTOR

Have the children make a paper caterpillar. Prepare ahead of time six different colors of 4"x4" pieces of construction paper, stapled together in two stacks of three pieces of paper each. Give each child two stacks of the 4"x4" colored construction paper, so that all the children have a total of six different colors of paper.

First have the children trace a circle using a template on each of their two stacks of construction paper. Then have them cut out the circles. Next, the children copy a pre made model to sequence the circles in the correct order to make a caterpillar; have them glue the circles onto a large piece of paper. The children also copy the model to draw in eyes, antennae, mouth, feet (2 per circle, except the head circle), and a triangle on the tail circle.

This activity may be modified by having the circles precut and/or giving the children a sheet of paper with highlighted circles (of the same colors of the circles) for them to match. You can also break the sequencing of the circles down and have the children place them individually by color, starting from left to right.

Materials
- Several 10" colored paper circle spots
- Pictures of different bugs
- 2 fly swatters
- Tape
- Magnifying glasses
- Crawling tunnel
- Balance beam
- 2-3 hula-hoops
- 2 nets with a handle
- 2 beanbags
- 2 balloons blown up
- Insect/caterpillar book (see suggestions under Cool-Down)
- Scissors – 1 for each child
- Glue – 1 for each child
- Circle shape templates for tracing – 1 for each child
- 6 different colors of 4"x4" pieces of construction paper – 1 color for each child
- Stapler
- Large white construction paper – 1 for each child

Team: *Diane Merlin, Loraine Ryan, Suzanne Cruz, Karen Steffens, TeriSue McEnery, Marjorie Swanson*

THEME: LAUNDRY

LESSON PLAN (QUICK VIEW)

1. **Warm-Up:** T-shirt relay race or "This Is the Way We Put on Our Clothes" action song
2. **Vestibular:** Steamroller and Sit 'n Spin™
3. **Proprioception:** Wash and wring clothes
4. **Balance:** Clothesline walk – picking up clothespins
5. **Eye-Hand Coordination:** Match and toss socks
6. **Cool-Down:** Laundry/clothes book
7. **Fine-Motor:** Sewing

1. WARM-UP

Have children form teams of 4-5. Have teams stand in a single file and "race" each other by having each child take a turn putting on and taking off a large t-shirt and passing it to the next child in line. The first team to finish wins.

Another option is to have the children sing the following song and complete the associated tasks.
(Sung to: Here we go around the "Mulberry Bush")

This is the way we put on our pants. (Put larger pants on over clothes)
Put on our pants.
Put on our pants.
This is the way we put on our pants so early in the morning.

Verse #2: This is the way we put on our shirt. (Put larger shirt on over clothes)
Verse #3: This is the way we put on our socks. (Put a pair of socks on over their socks)
Verse #4: This is the way we take off our pants. (Take larger pants off)
Verse #5: This is the way we take off our shirt. (Take off larger shirt)
Verse #6: This is the way we take off our socks. (Take off larger pair of socks)

2. VESTIBULAR

Explain to the children the task of washing and drying clothes. Have them take turns "going into the washing machine" (steamroller or sandwiched between two bolsters). While they go through the steamroller, spray them with a spray bottle. Next, have children go into the "dryer" (Sit 'n Spin). Turn on box fan to blow on them while spinning.

Note: Explain to the children that it is dangerous to repeat this activity at home using a real washer and dryer.

3. PROPRIOCEPTION

Fill a large plastic tub with water and children's bubble bath to give it a sudsy look. Fill the empty detergent bottle full with water. Have children take turns pouring from the detergent bottle to a specified line on a measuring cup and into the tub. Next, give each child an article of clothing to "wash." Have children wring out the clothing using both hands when they have finished washing. Encourage them to squeeze firmly.

4. BALANCE

Keeping the tub in place, hang a clothesline at a level the children can reach. Lay another clothesline along the floor leading from the tub to the first clothesline. Spread clothespins on the floor on either side of the clothesline. Have children walk on the clothesline squatting to pick up clothespins along the way. Have children take turns pinning their wet clothing on the clothesline.

5. EYE-HAND COORDINATION

Spread out unpaired socks on the floor. Have children match pairs of socks and toss the matched pairs into a laundry basket placed several feet away.

6. COOL-DOWN

Read a book related to laundry/clothes such as one of the following.
- *Fox in Socks* by Dr. Seuss (Random House, Inc., 1965)
- *Caillou – The Missing Sock* by Sarah Margaret Johnson (Chouette Publishing, 2003)
- *Froggy Gets Dressed* by Jonathan London; illustrated by Frank Remkiewicz (Penguin Books, 1992)

7. FINE-MOTOR

Have children sew together two pieces of fabric using a running stitch to make a "pocket."

> **Curriculum Suggestion:** A math lesson may be taught here easily. Doing the laundry typically includes folding it. In primary math classes, the geometry standard includes a benchmark for geometric figures and their properties. Students must recognize geometric shapes and describe their properties using concrete objects in a variety of situations. They should be able to demonstrate how a plane figure (square, rectangle, triangle, etc.) can be separated and/or combined to form an additional or a different geometric shape. By having the children fold their laundry – felt cloth or another material that has been cut in special geometric shapes – and experiment with different folds, they will be addressing and, most likely, mastering this benchmark. Instruct the students to do some estimating before they begin to fold the laundry. Supply an actual clothes basket full of towels and washcloths of various sizes. Students can touch them, wad them up, dig into the basket, etc. Ask them to

write down an estimate of how many towels and/or washcloths they predict are in the basket. After everyone has made an estimate, distribute the "clothes" to different teams of students. Let them explore folding and refolding the laundry.

Discuss the students' discoveries after about 5-10 minutes. For example, they should have noticed that the towels were specially cut shapes. Some will probably already have folded some of them into new squares, cones, triangles, etc. Let the class discussion lead to a brainstorming session about how many different shapes can be created from the ones provided.

Materials

- Large t-shirts
- 2 large bolsters or steamroller
- Spray bottle
- Sit 'n Spin™
- Box fan
- Large plastic tub
- Children's bubble bath
- Empty detergent bottle/measuring cup
- Clothes to wash
- 2 clotheslines and clothespins
- Pairs of socks to match
- Laundry basket
- Laundry/clothes book (see suggestions under Cool-Down)
- Pieces of fabric
- Needles/thread

Team: *Tisha DeGross, Lisa Loving*

THEME: MARDI GRAS OR 100TH SCHOOL DAY

LESSON PLAN (QUICK VIEW)

1. *Warm-Up:* Mardi Gras/100th school day book
2. *Vestibular:* "Second Line" dance with streamers
3. *Proprioception:* Mardi Gras parade
4. *Balance:* Mardi Gras relay
5. *Eye-Hand Coordination:* Beanbag toss
6. *Cool-Down:* "I'm Thinking of Something" game
7. *Fine-Motor:* King cake cinnamon rolls

1. WARM-UP

Read a book about Mardi Gras to acquaint the children with Mardi Gras and things associated with Mardi Gras. You could also celebrate the 100th school day and read a book about the 100th day of school. Suggested books include:

- *Mimi's First Mardi Gras* by Alice W. Couvillon; illustrated by Elizabeth Moore (Pelican Publishing Company, Inc., 1992) (These authors have written other books on this subject using the same characters.)
- *On Mardi Gras Day* by Fatima Shaik (Dial Books for Young Readers, 1999)
- *The Night Before the 100th Day of School* by Natasha Wing; illustrated by Mindy Pierce (Penguin Young Readers Group, 2005)
- *100th Day Worries* by Margery Cuyler; illustrated by Arthur Howard (Simon & Schuster Children's Publishing, 2005)

> **Curriculum Suggestion:** The festive atmosphere of Mardi Gras is a great entree to celebrating something about school. This lesson may be conducted around the time of the 100th day of school! This is traditionally a big deal for children in K-2. A parade could be arranged throughout the school. Young children could be assigned to hold the 100-day float, containing 100 pictures and/or words on butcher paper that the kids have learned so far in the year. There could be a 100 float for each subject area! On the math float there could be math words and symbols, the literacy float could display parts of speech, types of words – contractions, compounds, synonyms, antonyms, homophones, etc. – or titles of books the students have read.

2. VESTIBULAR

Give children streamers in Mardi Gras colors (yellow, green, and purple). Have them do a "Second Line" dance around the room. Children form a line and walk around the room waving streamers up and down. Tell them to try not to touch the ground. Play Mardi Gras music (Ultimate Mardi Gras; amazon.com).

3. PROPRIOCEPTION
Hold a Mardi Gras parade with scooter boards and wagons. Some children sit in the wagons or on the boards while others pull or push. Children throw beaded necklaces to classmates or children in other classes, just like during Mardi Gras.

4. BALANCE
Hold a Mardi Gras relay and have children walk on a balance beam in teams. Put a bucket of Mardi Gras beaded necklaces at one end and an empty bucket at the other. Children take turns picking up a beaded necklace and walking on the beam to the other side, then stoop and put the necklace in the other bucket and walk back. See which team transports all the necklaces first.

5. EYE-HAND COORDINATION
Divide children into two rows facing each other. Children throw beanbags in Mardi Gras colors (representing Mardi Gras beaded necklaces) to each other in pairs to simulate the "Throw me something mister" Mardi Gras tradition. After throwing back and forth once, children take one step back and throw again. If a team drops its beanbag, it is eliminated from the game. Continue to have the children step back until only one pair is left.

6. COOL-DOWN
Play "I'm Thinking of Something About Mardi Gras" game. Give clues for the children to solve. Discuss the different symbols of Mardi Gras and show pictures to illustrate. Possible riddles: Mardi Gras beads, floats, masks, parades, king cake, Mardi Gras colors, city where Mardi Gras is celebrated, Fat Tuesday, Mardi Gras Indians.

7. FINE-MOTOR
Have the children make their own king cake with cinnamon rolls and colored sugar. Use one cinnamon roll per child. Unroll the rolls of dough into strips. Then twist and make a circle. Cook and cool. Have the children spread icing on each roll and sprinkle with yellow, green, and purple sugar.

Materials
- Yellow, green, and purple streamers
- Mardi Gras beaded necklaces in different colors
- Mardi Gras or 100th school day book (see suggestions under Warm-Up)
- Mardi Gras CD music – Ultimate Mardi Gras (2001)
- Yellow, green, and purple small beanbags
- Balance beam
- Buckets
- Scooter boards and wagons
- Packaged unbaked cinnamon rolls
- Yellow, green, and purple sugar or food coloring to dye sugar

Team: *Gayle Pounds, Faith Rickert, Pam Hoffmann, Jennifer Landry, Suzette Howe*

THEME: OUTER SPACE

LESSON PLAN (QUICK VIEW)

1. **Warm-Up: 2001:** A Space Odyssey comet dance
2. **Vestibular:** Planets moving around the sun
3. **Proprioception:** Asteroids colliding
4. **Balance:** Moonwalk on stepping stones
5. **Eye-Hand Coordination:** Black hole balloon/ball toss
6. **Cool-Down:** Outer space or planet book
7. **Fine-Motor:** Rocket ship art project

1. WARM-UP

Give each student a yellow, red, or orange crepe paper streamer. Play a recording of *2001: A Space Odyssey* while the students move around the room like comets. Repeat several times.

> **Curriculum Suggestion:** For very young students, the color words corresponding to the streamers may be placed around the room and students could be instructed to use the color of their streamer to touch the matching color word. Students could trade colors and repeat several times.
>
> Older students may discuss details about planets, comets, and stars. Use visual aids to facilitate dialogue.

2. VESTIBULAR

Have students sit in a large circle (solar system). Give 2-3 students large balls (planets) and encourage them to rotate, twirling around the inside of the circle while the other students sit and watch. Have them circle around 3-4 times and then trade places with other students. Be sure they twirl in both directions. Continue until all students have had an opportunity to participate.

3. PROPRIOCEPTION

Using 2-3 beanbag chairs, divide the students into small groups and have them take turns jumping into the beanbags. (Asteroids crashing into planets.)

4. BALANCE

Place stepping-stones around the room for students to step on while pretending to moon walk.

> **Curriculum Suggestion:** Students may also use "eggshell mattress pads" to simulate the weightlessness idea of walking on the moon.

5. EYE-HAND COORDINATION

Wrap black crepe paper streamers taped around 2-3 hula-hoops to represent a black hole. Divide students into groups and direct them to toss balloons or nerf balls into the hula-hoops.

> **Curriculum Suggestion:** Hula-hoops may be labeled with different numbers, letters, word families, or fact families for students to practice and apply curriculum objectives in these areas.

6. COOL-DOWN

Read a book about outer space or planets such as one of the following. In preparation, place fluorescent stars and planets around the room. After the story, turn off the lights and have the children use a flashlight to find stars and planets.
- *Looking at the Planets: A Book About the Solar System* by Melvin Berger (Tandem Library Books, 1995)
- *Planet Earth/Inside Out* by Gail Gibbons (HarperCollins Publishers, 1998)

> **Curriculum Suggestion:** Write numbers, letters, words, or phonemic word families or word clusters on the stars/planets. Use the flashlights to shine on different numbers, etc., on the stars or planets. Instruct the students to "find all the numbers that add up to 10" or to locate all the words in the -ar word family.

7. FINE-MOTOR

Using construction paper, foam, or "cornstruction" paper (available at www.nuudles.com) shapes, make a rocket ship. Use a large rectangle, three circles for portholes, right-angle triangles for boosters, and an isosceles triangle for a nose cone. Have students glue the rectangle onto a piece of black construction paper. Place circles and triangles on the rectangle to make the rocket.

Note: "Cornstruction" paper requires no glue; just wet and place. To finish the rocket, add orange streamers at the bottom and sticker stars around the outside.

Materials
- Tape or CD player
- Tape or CD of *2001: A Space Odyssey*
- Crepe paper streamers in black, red, orange, and yellow
- Balls of various weights
- 2 or 3 large beanbags
- 2 or 3 hula-hoops
- Stepping-stones, enough to make a path
- Outer space or planet book (see suggestions under Cool-Down)
- Fluorescent stars and planets
- Flashlights
- Shapes in desired medium – construction paper, foam, or "cornstruction" paper
- Black construction paper, 1 per student
- Glue
- Sticky stars

Team: *Barb Stiman, Susan M. Wilkinson, Lee Ann Lorenzon, S. Hanson*

THEME: PIGS

LESSON PLAN (QUICK VIEW)

1. **Warm-Up:** "Old McDonald Had a Farm"
2. **Vestibular:** Hay rolling
3. **Proprioception:** "Haymow" jump
4. **Balance:** Pigsty balance beam
5. **Eye-Hand Coordination:** Corncob toss to pigs
6. **Cool-Down:** Pig book
7. **Fine-Motor:** Corncob art

1. WARM-UP

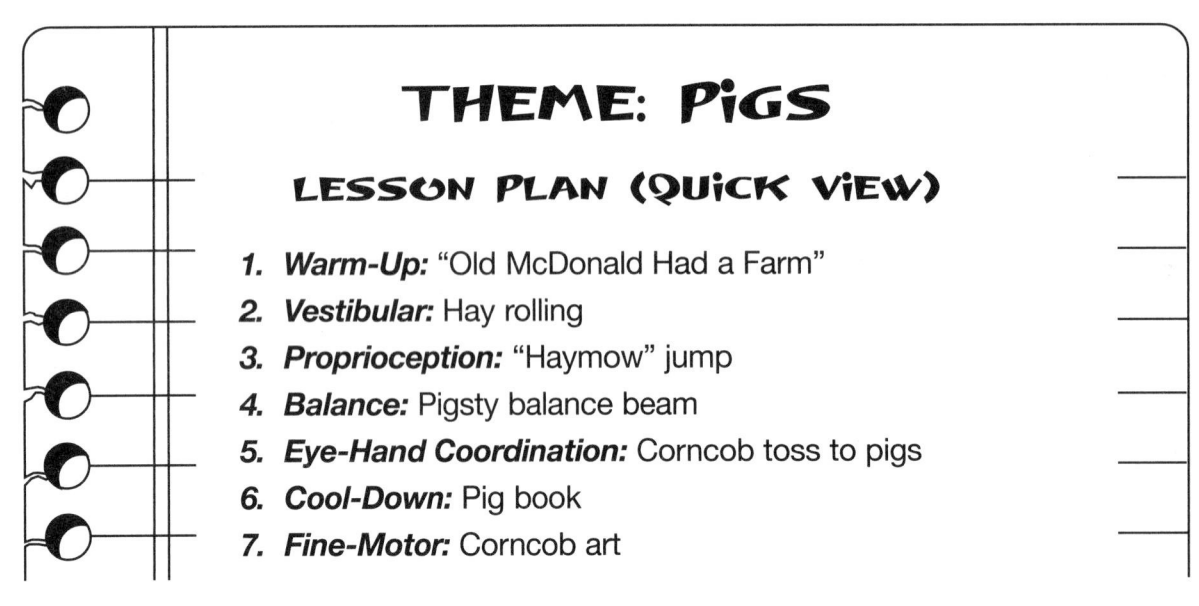

Have the children sing the following song and perform the animal sounds according to visual cards provided to them. Make sure to clearly enunciate E-I-E-I-O for oral motor exercise.

"Old McDonald Had a Farm"

Old McDonald had a farm
E-I-E-I-O
And on that farm he had a cow
E-I-E-I-O
With a moo-moo here
And a moo-moo there
Here a moo, there a moo
Everywhere a moo-moo.
Old McDonald had a farm
E-I-E-I-O

Verse #2: Sheep (Baa, baa)
Verse #3: Cat (Meow)
Verse #4: Dog (Woof, woof)
Verse #5: Horse (Neigh)
Verse #6: Pig (Oink, oink)

2. VESTIBULAR

Lay hay or yellow paper shredded into strips on a mat on the floor. Have the children lie down and log roll across the paper to pretend they are "rolling in the hay." Have them take two turns, rolling once in one direction and then back in the opposite direction.

3. PROPRIOCEPTION

Have the children pretend they are jumping in the haymow. Have them jump off a chair or step into a beanbag chair. Show the children a picture of a barn as some of them may not be familiar with a barn or a farm.

4. BALANCE
Have the children walk on a balance beam through the pretend pigsty. Ask them to reach down and pick up cobs of corn as they walk across the beam. Encourage them to try to bend down and reach for the cobs of corn without getting dirty by falling into the pigsty.

5. EYE-HAND COORDINATION
Have the children throw the cobs of corn they picked up from the balance beam activity into a pretend trough. Grade this activity by having the children start closer to the trough and gradually stepping farther and farther away.

6. COOL-DOWN
Read a book about pigs such as one of the following:
- *Mrs. Piggle Wiggle's Farm* by Betty MacDonald (HarperCollins Publishers, 1985)
- *Pigsty* by Mark Teague (Scholastic Inc, 1994)

7. FINE-MOTOR
Make pictures of corn on the cob using real corn kernels or pieces of unpopped popcorn. Have the children glue down the kernels on a picture of a corncob. Encourage a nice pincer grasp on each kernel to glue it in place on the picture.

> **Curriculum Suggestion:** Tell the students they will be doing math with the corn before they glue it down. To address math benchmarks for place value, skip counting, multiplication readiness, etc., give each child or group a cup of corn kernels. Model how to divide kernels into groups of tens and leftovers. Show the students how to skip count by tens to find the total. Following this, request that they exchange their kernels for a concrete object representing the number of kernels they have counted – base ten blocks. These manipulatives make it easy to visualize the base ten number system and to count by tens because the tens are connected. Once the students understand how to group the blocks and use them to count the number of kernels they had, use them to introduce and teach adding and subtracting with them.

Materials
- Mat
- Hay or yellow paper shredded into strips
- Chair, step, or platform to jump from
- Large beanbag chair
- Balance beam
- Cobs of corn
- Box or laundry basket for a pretend trough
- Pig book (see suggestions under Cool-Down)
- Glue
- Corn kernels or un-popped popcorn
- Photocopied pictures of corncobs

Team: *Renee Ades, Robin Schwab, Kay Nigbor, Leah Crull, Terri Steinhaus, Heidi Baumgartner, Tracy Boyer, Dianne Hendrickson*

THEME: POLICE

LESSON PLAN (QUICK VIEW)

1. **Warm-Up:** Police book
2. **Vestibular:** "Red light, green light"/spin and sound like siren
3. **Proprioception:** Police academy calisthenics
4. **Balance:** Walk on police tape/stay inside "crosswalk"
5. **Eye-Hand Coordination:** Beanbag toss/catch in police hats
6. **Cool-Down:** "Blowouts" (party toys) for pretend police whistles
7. **Fine-Motor:** Draw outline of child's body

1. WARM-UP

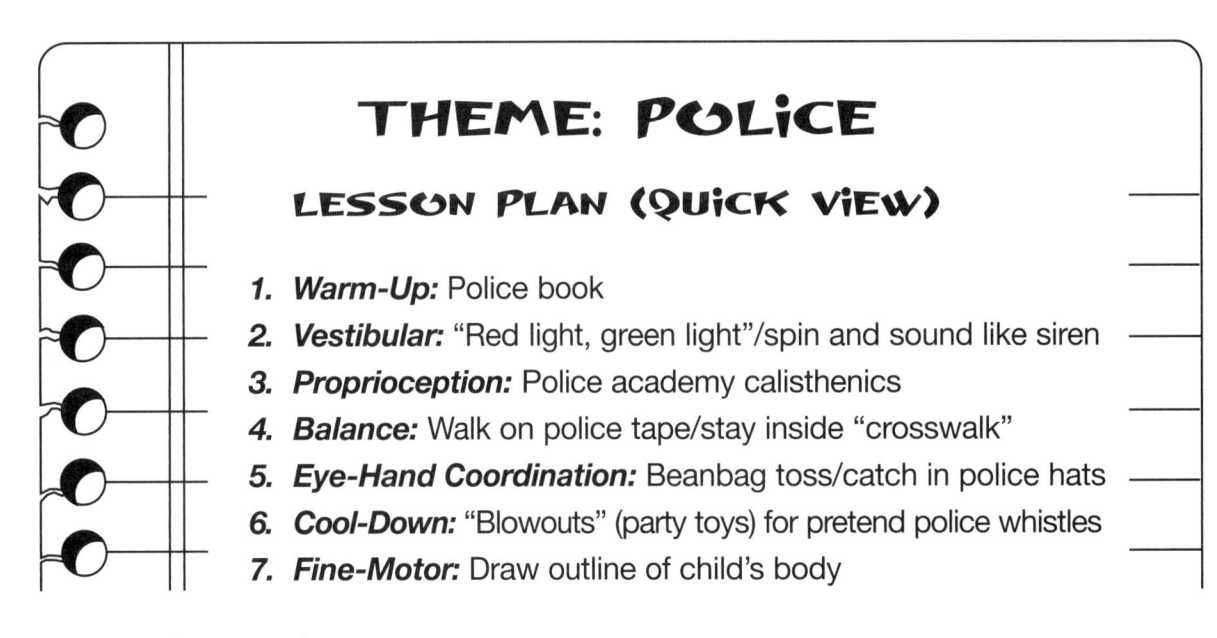

Read a book about police such as one of the following. Talk about police uniforms, special tools, and fingerprinting. Look at all the places a police officer helps us (school, police station, traffic).

- *I'm Going to Be a Police Officer* by Edith Kunhardt (Scholastic, 1995)
- *A Day at the Police Station* by Richard Scarry (Golden Books, 2004)

2. VESTIBULAR

Play "Red light, green light" with the teacher as the traffic signal. If the teacher says, "green light," students may take steps forward. If the teacher says, "red light," all students must stop walking forward. Any students who keep walking are out and have to sit down.

> **Curriculum Suggestion:** To incorporate another modality, write the words *red* and *green* on paper or use red and green pieces of paper. Rather than saying "red or green light," hold up the sign or the colored paper. This makes the activity a visual and color identification activity.

Optional Activity: Children can also spin around and make the siren noise. Talk about the fact that a police car sounds a siren to let people know it is coming. Sometimes a police car has to go very fast (chase) or very slowly (procession/parade), so change the speed of the spinning.

Note: Be sure to go in both directions when spinning.

3. PROPRIOCEPTION

Tell the children they are going to train to be police officers. Give each child a star badge to wear. Have the children trace a star shape and write the word POLICE on it. Tell the students that the police exercise to stay healthy. They must stay in good shape to be able to run, climb, or jump to help people. They go to a special school called the Police Academy. At the academy they do exercises. Exercise with the children by doing jumping jacks, sit-ups, jogging in place or around the room, stretching, and touching toes.

> **Curriculum Suggestion:** This is good time to introduce geometric shapes that children are expected to master at their individual grade levels: circles, squares, rectangles, triangles, and ellipses. Provide the shapes and instruct the children to make unique police badges in different shapes than the star. Lines of symmetry, also part of K-2 math standards and benchmarks, may be learned and practiced with each shape. The children can sort and classify these and other shapes into groups of "symmetrical" or "not symmetrical."

4. BALANCE

Tell the children that the police use special tape to keep people safe and away from dangerous situations. Use the yellow caution tape to make a line on the floor, leading to the police station. You can make the police station ahead of time. Use a refrigerator box and cut out a door and window. Write or paint "Police Station" on the box. Ask the children to walk on the lines to the police station. Music may be playing in the background.

5. EYE-HAND COORDINATION

Divide the students into two groups. Place a police hat in front of each group at a distance appropriate for the students' skill level. Give children three beanbags to toss into the police hat. Repeat until all children have had a turn.

> **Curriculum Suggestion:** Upgrade the activity to integrate a communication or math curriculum benchmark. Hats may be labeled with different words, letters, numerals, word families, rhyming words, etc. Instruct the children to aim their beanbag into the hat (a) that rhymes with a word you are studying, (b) that is labeled with a letter or number that is being learned, or (c) that shows the correct sum to a math fact that you announce. The list of ideas for this activity is endless.

6. COOL-DOWN

Give children their own "blowout" party toy as pretend police whistles and have them practice blowing.

7. FINE-MOTOR

Divide the children into pairs. Have one child lie down on a piece of newsprint. The other student traces around the first child's body. Have them switch roles so that each child has an outline of his or her body. Let the children add details to their outlines such as hair, face, and clothing.

Materials
- Police book (see suggestions under Warm-Up)
- Yellow caution tape
- Plastic police hats
- Beanbags
- Cutout paper stars
- Large roll of newsprint
- Refrigerator box to make into a police station
- Toy handcuffs
- Markers
- Blowout party toys – one for each child

Team: *Jill Hermansen, Barbara Magera, Jackie Pederson, Lucky Peterson, Jessica Evenson*

THEME: PUPPIES

LESSON PLAN (QUICK VIEW)

1. **Warm-Up:** "Bingo" action song
2. **Vestibular:** Puppy games – jump the fence
3. **Proprioception:** Sock tug of war
4. **Balance:** Puppy "beg" for a treat
5. **Eye-Hand Coordination:** Pretend puppy Frisbee catch
6. **Cool-Down:** Puppy book
7. **Fine-Motor:** Puppy mask

1. WARM-UP

Have the children sing the familiar song "Bingo."

There was a farmer had a dog and Bingo was his name oh,
B-I-N-G-O, B-I-N-G-O, B-I-N-G-O and Bingo was his name oh.
There was a farmer had a dog and Bingo was his name oh.
(Clap hands in place of the letter B) I-N-G-O, (clap hands in place of the letter B) I-N-G-O,
(Clap hands in place of the letter B) I-N-G-O and Bingo was his name oh.
Repeat song until all letters of "Bingo" are replaced with a clap.

2. VESTIBULAR

Create three "fences" out of masking tape on the floor. The first should measure 12 inches in width, the second, 24 inches in width, and the third, 36 inches in width. Have the children start at the first fence and jump over it, proceeding to the next fence and then the last fence.

3. PROPRIOCEPTION

Explain to the children that puppies like to play with socks, pulling on them with their mouth and paws. Pair the children with a partner and give each pair a tube sock. Have children hold their end of the sock with a tight hand grasp and tell them they need to try to pull the sock away form their partner.

> **Curriculum Suggestion:** For this phonemic awareness activity, provide a tube sock for each student to stretch. Explain to the students that they will be stretching their tube sock by grasping each end of the sock and pulling them in opposite directions. As they stretch the sock, they are pretending to be stretching like a puppy. Say some simple words such as current spelling words, word wall words, word of the day list, vocabulary words, etc. The student repeats the words while stretching his sock.

> For another activity, say a word that has a vowel sound in the medial position. The students stretch the word out at the vowel position while simultaneously stretching the sock. Hold the vowel sound with your voice to distinguish its sound from other sounds during the sock stretching. Example for a word like *pup*: <begin slowly stretching – pronounce initial /p/, then /u-u-u-u-u-u-u-u-u/ while stretching, hold the /u/ sound, then release the stretch and pronounce the final consonant letter /p/.

4. BALANCE

Have the children stay in pairs. Tell them to pretend they are puppies begging for a treat. Have them either stand on their tip-toes or on one leg. Challenge them to see who can stand in the chosen position the longest.

5. EYE-HAND COORDINATION

Have the children remain in their pairs. Ask them to start out by standing 2 feet apart and have them toss the ball/Frisbee to each other. Each time they catch the Frisbee/ball, they can take a step back to increase the distance between them.

> **Curriculum Suggestion:** While the students toss the ball/frisbee back and forth, instruct them to practice any of the following:
> - Skip counting by 2s, 5s, 10s, 20s, etc. (depending on grade-level outcome); coin or bill values: penny, nickel, quarter, half dollar, ones, fives, tens, etc.
> - Spelling word recitation – d-o-g
> - Multiple-syllabic word or compound word practice (each toss would be worth one syllable. Ex: Fris/bee = two tosses)
> - Simple math fact practice; ex: 2 + 2 = 4. This would be worth five tosses back and forth
>
> Be creative and develop additional activities.

> **Curriculum Suggestion:** Instruct students to lengthen what they say while the Frisbee or ball is in flight; ex: How far can you get in the alphabet while the Frisbee/ball is in the air? Throw – a, b, c, d, e, f, g, h, i, j, k, l, ... catch. Repeat the procedure with other suggestions. Ex: Throw – 2, 4, 6, 8, 10, 12, 14, 16, 18, ... catch.

6. COOL-DOWN

Read a book about puppies such as one of those listed below. Discuss the importance of taking care of and playing with pets. Ask the children what they would do to help take care of their pets at home and what kind of games they would play with their pet.

- *Just Me and My Puppy* by Mercer Mayer (Golden Books, 1998)
- *Poor Puppy* by Nick Bruel (Roaring Brook Press, 2007)

7. FINE-MOTOR

Give each child a paper plate to make into a puppy mask. Have the children cut eye-holes in the plate, trace noses and ears on construction paper and cut them out to paste on, and draw a mouth and spots for their puppy face. Finally, they can staple on an elastic or paper strap to secure the mask around their head.

> **Curriculum Suggestion:** Standard 3 in writing states, "The students write effectively for a variety of audiences, purposes, and contexts." Use this opportunity to explore grammar and parts of speech for proper word choice in writing.
>
> Using an overhead projector to model, show how to draw a simple picture of a pup using as few steps as possible. Next, have the children write the word *pup*. Once they have copied each of the steps, draw a line to connect the picture to the word. Label it as a Pup and put a circle around the word. Explain that the word *pup* is a noun. Ask students to name parts of the pup's body. As they do so, label each part by writing a name and putting circle around each word to identify it as a noun. This may be all that can be completed at this point for the first day.
>
> At the next available instruction time, explain that the students will now learn about verbs. Ask the class to tell something that the parts of the pup's body can do. The tail can wag. The tongue can lick. The legs can run or jump. Draw a line to connect the name of the body part to the action that it can do. Write ONLY the word – *jump, run, lick, wag*, etc. Draw a line under the words and tell the class these words are verbs – words that show actions.

Have the students follow your modeling and complete the same spelling and labeling that you do.

Materials
- Masking tape
- Cotton tube socks – one for each child
- Tennis balls or Frisbees
- Puppy book (see suggestions under Cool-Down)
- Paper plate for each child
- Paper or elastic band for mask
- Construction paper to trace noses and ears; black for the noses and white for the ears
- Scissors, paste, crayons, stapler

Team: *Kylie Long, Joyce Boo, Ellen Frankino*

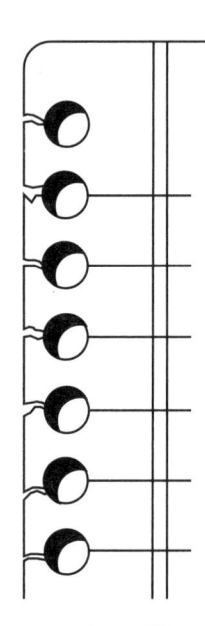

THEME: SNOW

LESSON PLAN (QUICK VIEW)

1. **Warm-Up:** Snow book
2. **Vestibular:** Sledding down a ramp/hallway on scooters
3. **Proprioception:** Ski lift with tow rope
4. **Balance:** Ice skating
5. **Eye-Hand Coordination:** Snowball fight, homemade ice cream
6. **Cool-Down:** Snow angels, draw-a-snowman
7. **Fine-Motor:** Paper snowflakes

1. WARM-UP

Have the children gather in a semi-circle, sitting with legs crossed, and listen to a book about snow such as one of those listed below.

- *The Snowflake: A Water Cycle Story* by Neil Waldman (Lerner Publishing Group, 2003)

> **Curriculum Suggestion:** This book is well suited to be integrated into a science or language arts unit at any grade level. The words are wonderful and could be a springboard for poetry, word choice in 6 Trait Writing, or just to enjoy.

- *Snowflake Bentley* by Jacqueline Briggs Martin (Houghton Mifflin Company, 1998)
- *Millions of Snowflakes* by Mary McKenna Siddals (Houghton Mifflin Company, 1998)

> **Curriculum Suggestion:** This counting book can easily be used to create a counting book about snowflakes or to introduce place value vocabulary for math: millions.

> **Curriculum Suggestion:** Apply the science process skills of predicting and testing a hypothesis. Have students make snowballs of three sizes at recess. Place them in Ziploc™ bags. Have students predict how long it will take for the different-sized snowballs to melt. Record their predictions on a graph in one color. Assign a student or team of students to time how long it takes for the snowballs to actually melt. Record the results on the graph in another color. Compare and discuss the findings. Instruct students to record this process in a science journal or notebook. They can also illustrate the procedure.

2. VESTIBULAR

If your school has a ramp, have the children walk quietly to the ramp and use a scooter to slide down the ramp, or walk with their feet if the ramp is too steep. You may also use carpet pieces for the children to slide on and push themselves with their arms to the bottom. If your school does not have a ramp, have the children scoot down the hallway using the same motions.

3. PROPRIOCEPTION

Line the children up at one end of the hall. Have them take turns lying prone (on their stomach) on a scooter board or carpet square and pull hand over hand along a rope that is secured by an adult at the other end of the hall. They are to pretend they are being pulled by a tow rope up a mountain to ski down. You may want to show them pictures of a towrope and a chair lift so they will have some prior knowledge.

> **Curriculum Suggestion:** Maximize this activity by hanging words, letters, math facts, numbers, parts of speech, etc., on the rope after the students have completed the course once. Tell them to do the same again, but this time whenever they reach a card with something written on it, they must shout out the word, sum (if it is an addition fact), whether or not it is odd or even, or whether it is a noun, verb, adjective, etc.
>
> Instruct older students to pair with someone. Give one student a clipboard and a sheet of paper. This student must write the words, numbers, etc., down for the partner. When the child on the scooter gets back to the end, tell both of them they must unscramble the words they found to make a sentence or a math problem, etc.

4. BALANCE

Prepare the following ahead of time. Tear wax paper (two sheets per child) to the size of the child's foot. Have the children place one piece of wax paper under each foot. Demonstrate before you start how to push off with your feet, DON'T LIFT YOUR FEET. Keep your feet flat on the ground, and skate around the room. Play music while they skate.

> **Curriculum Suggestion:** A standard in science is to understand properties of different objects and observe and record how one object interacts with another object (Standard 2). Prior to the skating activity, tell the students to observe different types of paper, foil, cloth, plastic wrap, metal, or material, etc. Include wax paper as one type. Tell students to list the properties (may have to introduce this term early on) of the different materials. List their suggestions on the board or overhead. Have the students predict which type of "skate" slides the easiest. Discuss their reasoning. (Older students can write their predictions in their science journals and give their reasons for what they choose.) Next, have them test their predictions and discuss their findings. A discussion of forces should lead to the introduction of the word *friction*. If not, suggest that they repeat the skating, removing their shoes this time. A discussion about the heat they feel is a great way to introduce friction – a force that acts on all moving objects.

Lesson Themes 125

> Conclude with the idea that the wax paper produces the least friction and, therefore, is the best one to use as a "skate."

5. EYE-HAND COORDINATION

Hold a snowball fight. Have the children crumple up pieces of typing paper to form balls. Each child can make 5-10 balls. Place a rope in the center of the room. Divide the children in two groups and have one group stand on one side and the other group on the other side of the rope. They are to listen for the signal word *freeze* (to indicate start and stop). The children must throw the balls overhand toward the other side of the rope.

Note: Emphasize throwing the "snowball" below the head to avoid hitting somebody in the eyes.

Alternate Activity: Make homemade ice cream. Mix the ingredients prior to class (see instructions below). Have the children sit in a circle and toss the bag of ice cream to the person next to them for 5-10 minutes until the ice cream is formed. Serve a small amount of ice cream to each child in a small paper cup, either immediately after the activity or freeze it and serve later in the day.

Note: As always, check for children's food sensitivities/allergies.

6. COOL-DOWN

Have the children make pretend snow angels on the floor. Then have them sit at their desks and design a snowman on paper with their crayons. Ask the children what they want to be when they grow up and create a unique snowman to match their dreams, such as a rock musician snowman, ballerina snowman, basketball player snowman, etc.

7. FINE-MOTOR

Have the students make paper snowflakes. Have them fold a piece of 8" x 11" paper up into triangles and halves. Then have them snip triangles or half circles along the edges of their folded paper. Have the children unfold the paper to discover their one-of-a-kind snowflake.

> **Curriculum Suggestion:** Take students outside on a snowy day, if appropriate. Provide them with a magnifying glass and a piece of black construction paper. Instruct them to allow snowflakes to fall on their black paper and observe the structure of the flakes. Divide students into pairs so one can write down their findings. "The Snowflake Catcher" can announce to the "Recorder" how many points are on the snowflakes and how many she sees that are similar. Once back inside, students can create a bar graph, data table, or other visual to illustrate different snowflakes that they collected or made. They can count how many five-, six-, seven-, etc., pointed snowflakes fell on their black paper. This is an easy way to integrate math and reading/interpreting data and charts.

Science process skills used include organizing, observing, classifying, collecting data, etc. A follow-up may be to "grow" their own crystals using borax or sugar in a classroom-controlled setting. See the following link for this activity, http://chemistry.about.com/cs/howtos/ht/boraxsnowflake.htm (may be done together in class at grades K-1 and with supervision at grade 2 and up).

Materials

- Snow book (see suggestions under Warm-Up)
- Scooter/carpet pieces
- Long rope
- Pictures of a towrope/chairlift
- Wax paper torn to the size of the children's feet (two per child)
- CD player/CDs with music to be played while skating
- Typing paper (a bundle) for the snowball fight, drawing a snowman character, and cutting out snowflakes
- Crayons, scissors
- Ingredients for making ice cream (This will serve 4-6 children, so you can have two to three groups going at a time. Prepare all before class.):
  - 1 cup whole milk
  - 1 cup Half and Half
  - 1/2 tsp vanilla
  - 2 pounds of ice
  - 1 cup coarse salt
  - 1 quart-sized freezer baggie
  - 1 gallon-sized freezer baggie
  - Duct tape
  - Small cup or bowl and spoon (one for each child)

Directions: Mix together the milk, Half and Half, and vanilla. Put it into the quart-size baggie. Duct tape the top shut so it will not leak. In the gallon-size baggie, put the salt, ice, and the quart-sized baggie with the mixture. Close and duct tape the gallon baggie shut so it will not leak. Wrap it in a towel if you are going to toss to a friend or place the baggies in a tin can and roll it back and forth. It takes about 15 minutes to firm up.

Team: *Sara Deitering, Heidi Larson, Anne Marie Johnson*

THEME: SNOWMAN

LESSON PLAN (QUICK VIEW)

1. **Warm-Up:** Book about snowmen
2. **Vestibular:** Pin the Carrot Nose on the Snowman/tumbling snowballs
3. **Proprioception:** Therapy ball snowman with partners
4. **Balance:** Scooter board snowboarding
5. **Eye-Hand Coordination:** Catch falling snowflakes; paper snowball catch
6. **Cool-Down:** "Frosty the Snowman" song
7. **Fine-Motor:** Candy snowman; paper snowman

1. WARM-UP

Read a book about snowmen such as one of those listed below. Discuss parts that are necessary to make a snowman using precut felt items, such as carrot nose, scarf, hat, buttons, white circles, etc.

Optional: Use a felt board to retell one of the snowman stories by having the children each have a turn assembling parts of the snowman with felt pieces.

- *The Biggest, Best Snowman* by Margery Cuyler (Scholastic, 2004)
- *All You Need for a Snowman* by Alice Schertle (Harcourt, 2007)
- *Snowmen at Night* by Caralyn Buehner (Dial, 2003)
- *Snowmen at Christmas* by Caralyn Buehner (Dial Books for Young Readers, 2005)
- *Snowman in a Box* by Nancy Armstrong (Perseus Publishing, 2004)

2. VESTIBULAR

Divide the class into two groups. Have one group play "Pin the Carrot Nose on the Snowman," with each child taking a turn at pinning the carrot nose on the snowman. (Make a large snowman ahead of time and hang on the wall/door at child level. Give each child a carrot nose with masking tape on the back.) If the children can tolerate being blindfolded, blindfold one child at a time or have them close their eyes. Give the child a nose and spin them around five times. Now have them try to place the carrot nose in the correct place on the snowman. Repeat this for each child and compare how close each child gets to the correct placement of the nose. Use a ruler to measure.

> **Curriculum Suggestion:** Capitalize on this activity by integrating place value practice while pinning the nose on the snowman. Instruct students to count by ones, tens, or hundreds (depending on grade level) while they are blindfolded and spun around. Instead of only having one snowman, create three (or more for an enrichment lesson) snowmen.

> Label each as follows: ones, tens, hundreds, etc., and label each carrot with a numeral between 1 and 9. Depending on where the student places the "carrot nose," her team/group gets 1 point, 10 points, or 100 points, 2 points, 20 points, or 200 points, etc. This way the students can see that numerals in different places are valued differently.

Engage the other group in the following activity. Prior to beginning this activity, teach the children how to make a snowman by rolling snowballs in the snow. Place a mat on the floor and have one child lie on the mat and perform a forward tumble as if she were rolling into a snowball. Have each child repeat this at least twice. The children may also try tumbling backward.

3. PROPRIOCEPTION

Continue with the "making a snowman" idea. Divide students into pairs. It is best to have two pairs going at the same time so the children receive more input and less downtime. Using large, heavy therapy balls, have two students roll the "snowball" around the room to pretend more snow is sticking to the ball. Have the partners pick up a large beanbag chair and place it in a designated spot. Then pick up the therapy ball, and place it on top of, but nestled into, the beanbag chair to build a snowman.

4. BALANCE

Under close supervision, have the children kneel on a skateboard or scooter board and hold onto a rope while an adult slowly pulls the child around a path as if he were snowboarding.

Another option would be to have the children walk across a balance beam placed on the floor while holding a child-sized shovel and pretending they are shoveling snow along the path. You may put cotton or cotton balls on the floor for them to pick up with the shovel as they walk across the beam.

5. EYE-HAND COORDINATION

This activity can be done in a couple of different ways. First, if you have a bubble machine, turn it on and have the bubbles blowing in the air. If not, use a container of bubbles to make bubbles. As the bubbles fall to the ground, have each child reach and poke the bubbles with their index finger and pop them before they land on the ground.

Another option is to use packing styrofoam peanuts. Toss several peanuts into the air and direct the children to catch as many "snowflakes" as they can.

In yet another version, tell the children that they will be making snowballs and that in order to make the perfect snowball you have to pack the snow into a ball. Give each child a piece of white paper. Have them crinkle and squeeze the paper into a ball shape. Have them find a partner and toss the snowballs back and forth to each other.

6. COOL-DOWN

Have the children sing the following song while seated. Make a large copy of the song for the children to follow along to work on their reading skills.

Frosty the Snowman

Frosty the Snowman
Was a jolly happy soul
With a corncob pipe and a button nose
And two eyes made out of coal

Frosty the Snowman
Is a fairytale they say
He was made of snow
But the children know
How he came to life one day

There must have been some magic
In that old silk hat they found
For when they placed it on his head
He began to dance around

Frosty the Snowman
Was alive as he could be
And the children say
He could laugh and play
Just the same as you and me

Frosty the Snowman
Knew the sun was hot that day
So he said let's run
And we'll have some fun
Now before I melt away

Down to the village
With a broomstick in his hand
Running here and there all around the square
Saying catch me if you can

He led them down the streets of town
Right to the traffic cop
And he only paused a moment when
He heard him holler stop

Frosty the Snowman
Had to hurry on his way
But he waved goodbye
Saying don't you cry
I'll be back again some day

Thumpety thump thump
Thumpety thump thump
Look at Frosty go
Thumpety thump thump
Thumpety thump thump
Over the hills of snow

7. FINE-MOTOR

Using the reproducible outline of a snowman, make a copy for each child on white construction paper. Have the children color the parts of the snowman (hat, nose, etc.), cut them out and glue the pieces together to make the snowman (have a sample snowman completed prior to the activity). They can use buttons or beads for eyes, mouth, and the snowman's buttons. For younger children, cut out the snowmen and put them together. Then have the students glue cotton balls onto the body of the snowmen and glue the eyes, nose, mouth, and buttons using the buttons or beads.

After the children have completed their snowmen, if time permits, have each child make a snowman using marshmallows and candy pieces that they can eat. To do so, connect three marshmallows using toothpicks to make the snowman's body. Using a small dab of white icing, attach M&Ms or some other small candy pieces for the eyes and buttons down the front of the body. Use pretzel sticks for the arms and a small piece of licorice for the mouth. After they have assembled their snowmen, the children can either save them to take home to eat or eat them right away.

Materials

- Book about a snowman (see suggestions under Warm-Up)
- Felt items for snowman (eyes, carrot nose, scarf, hat, buttons, sticks for arms)
- Felt board
- Large-size snowman taped to wall or door
- Orange construction paper carrot noses – one for each child
- Blindfold (optional)
- Masking tape
- Ruler
- Mat
- 2 large therapy balls
- 2 beanbag chairs
- Skateboard or scooter board
- Tow rope or jump rope
- Small shovel
- Cotton balls
- Bottle of bubbles or bubble machine
- Packing peanuts
- A piece of white paper – one for each child
- Large copy of "Frosty the Snowman" song
- Copies of snowman parts
- Crayons, scissors, glue
- Cotton balls
- Buttons or beads
- Marshmallows (3 for each child)
- Toothpicks
- Small candy pieces (M&Ms, cinnamon hearts, etc.)
- Pretzel sticks
- White icing
- Rope licorice

Team: *Kriss Staab, Tricia Thorman, Heather Hough, Alanna Bosley, Erin Moser*

Template for Snowman

Lesson Themes 133

THEME: SPRING FLOWERS

LESSON PLAN (QUICK VIEW)

1. *Warm-Up:* "Seed" action poem
2. *Vestibular:* Flowers blowing in the wind
3. *Proprioception:* Tug-of-war weed pull
4. *Balance:* Garden path walk
5. *Eye-Hand Coordination:* Watering flowers
6. *Cool-Down:* Spring flowers book
7. *Fine-Motor:* Seed/tissue paper flower picture

1. WARM-UP

Have the children say the following poem and perform the associated actions.

You are a tiny seed (Kids are curled up in fetal position)
Your roots sprout (Kids stretch feet out)
The sun comes out and you begin to grow (Hands start to go up)
The sun and rain make you stronger (Kids get into squat and slowly stand)
You are a beautiful flower (Stand up with hands over head)

2. VESTIBULAR

Talk to the children about flowers blowing in the wind. Have them stand up with arms out and move around the room like a flower blowing in the wind. Using a fan as the wind, instruct them to move when the fan is on and to stop when the fan is off. Have the children move a different way each time. For example, hopping, side slide, heel to toe, backward, crab walk, bear walk.

3. PROPRIOCEPTION

Discuss how weeds can be bad for new seeds and that weeds, therefore, should be pulled. Bring in some gardening gloves and have the children put them on. Place a long rope on the floor and tie a piece of material at the center. Divide the children into two groups, each group holding on to one end of the rope. Tell them the rope is a weed. When you say, "Go," the children pull on their end of the rope for 20-30 seconds. Have them rest and repeat several times.

4. BALANCE

Prepare an obstacle course consisting of stepping-stones and a balance beam. Arrange die-cut flowers on each side of the beam. Tell the children they are walking through a garden on stepping-stones. When they get to the beam, they are to walk across and "pick" a flower from the floor.

5. EYE-HAND COORDINATION

Bring in some potted flowers for the children to water using a watering can.

6. COOL-DOWN

Read a book about flowers such as one of the following. Discuss how to plant seeds and how they grow into flowers.
- *When the Wind Stops* by Charlotte Zolotow (HarperCollins Children's Books, 1997)
- *Grandma's Purple Flowers* by Adjoa J. Burrowes (Lee & Low Books, Inc., 2000)

> **Curriculum Suggestion:** After reading the story, instruct the students to pair up with one another and summarize what they think was happening in the story. After 2 minutes, tell them to stop. Choose several groups to discuss their findings with the class. This will initiate a discussion about a main idea of the story: wind.
>
> Using a fan, model how important wind is to help plants/flowers reproduce. Hold different varieties of seeds in front of the blowing fan. Measure the distance that each type of seed blows from the fan. Be sure to include some milkweed or similar seeds so the students will see that the light hairs on the seeds can help carry them for miles. Once you have modeled the activity, group the children into teams to complete it. Instruct them to gather data, organize them in a table, and create a graph of their results.

7. FINE-MOTOR

Give each child a picture of a flower. Have the children glue seeds onto the center of flower. An example of a free download flower picture may be found at: http://www.coloring-page.com/pages/sunflwr3.html

For more of a challenge, use bits of tissue paper to make a colorful purple flower to go along with the book *Grandma's Purple Flowers*. The children can form the tissue paper around the end of a pencil (eraser end), dip it in glue, and attach it to a cutout of a flower or a flower they have drawn. This makes a great finished product and is very tactile. Kids must use fine-motor control to manipulate, cut, and attach small pieces of tissue paper on an outline of a flower. This addresses eye-hand coordination, too.

Materials
- Fan
- Mat
- Gardening gloves (optional)
- Long rope
- Stepping-stones
- Balance beam
- Die-cut flowers
- Potted flowers
- Watering cans
- 8-1/2"x11" white paper with copy of flower
- Glue
- Seeds
- Purple tissue paper
- Spring flowers (see suggestions under Cool-Down)

Team: *Deb Moyer, Daphne Johnson, Karen Moe, Elisabeth Moe, Valerie Payne*

THEME: THE SNOWY DAY

LESSON PLAN (QUICK VIEW)

1. **Warm-Up:** *The Snowy Day* by Ezra Keats
2. **Vestibular:** Angels in the snow, snowball roll
3. **Proprioception:** Snowman "boxes" stack
4. **Balance:** Footprints walk in snow
5. **Eye-Hand Coordination:** Snowball throwing
6. **Cool-Down:** Pretend melting snowman
7. **Fine-Motor:** Snowflakes on window pane

1. WARM-UP

With the children sitting in a circle, read the book *The Snowy Day* by Ezra Keats. Have the children try on mittens, hats, scarves, or boots. Incorporate this into a relay-type race or "timed" event. (Put them on, take them off, and pass to the next child in line.) This dressing task may be incorporated into the school day before going outside on a cold, wintry day. Alternatively, sitting around an open window, the students could be enjoying some hot chocolate while trying on the scarves, mittens, etc.

- *The Snowy Day* by Ezra Jack Keats (Penguin Group, 1996)

Once the story has been read aloud, have the children act out the story for the second time. For example, putting on snowsuit, walking with toes pointing in and out, dragging a stick, etc. The children can do the motions to the specific key points of the story. Define the words *smacking, heaping, adventures* before reading the story and reinforce when you come to the words during the reading. At the beginning of the story, place a little bit of snow in a bowl. By the end of the second reading, it should have melted to demonstrate melting (science). (Contributed by Sara Deitering from "Snow" Team.)

2. VESTIBULAR

Teach the children how to lie on the floor and move their arms and legs to simulate making angels in the snow. Children can also curl up into snowballs by lying on their backs and holding their knees against their chests while also lifting their heads. Another idea is to have the children do a forward roll as if rolling a large snowball for a snowman.

3. PROPRIOCEPTION

Tell the children that they will be making a snowman. Use three weighted, graduated-sized boxes painted white that they can stack to make the body. Children can take turns sticking on paper eyes, buttons, nose, and mouth, as well as putting on a hat and scarf.

> **Curriculum Suggestion:** Use the boxes to introduce size comparisons in K-1, using terms like *small, smaller, smallest; large, larger, largest*, etc. Kids could predict (predicting is a science process skill) (and test) what would happen if snowmen were built upside down. Have the children pose with their completed "snowperson." Take their pictures and print them out. Allow each child to write or dictate a story, sentence, paragraph – whatever is appropriate for the grade level – to go with the pictures. Gather the pages and bind into a class book that can be checked out and read at home with family.

4. BALANCE

Tape white paper footprints (pretend "snow" footprints) in a circular pattern around the room. Have the children step on the snow footprints while maintaining their balance. Mix up the footprint walking pattern to create a challenge for older children. For example, make a hopscotch pattern, criss-cross pattern, backward pattern, sideways pattern, one-foot hopping pattern. Play music in the background.

5. EYE-HAND COORDINATION

Have the children throw white yarn balls or large marshmallows into a bucket. Another idea is to place sheets of typing paper on the floor and having the children use two hands to scoop up the paper and crumple it tightly into a "snowball.

6. COOL-DOWN

Have the children pretend they are snowmen and that the sun is getting hotter and hotter. As it gets hotter, they slowly melt down to the floor in a puddle.

7. FINE-MOTOR

Make a large cardboard window frame out of a corrugated box. Line the windows with "glass" made out of clear plastic report covers (available at an office supply store). Have the children stamp on snowflakes by using a white bingo marker or use a snowflake stencil and white paint to make the flakes. Snowflakes cut out of paper using a large craft punch may also be stuck to regular windows using double-stick tape.

Alternative Activity: Design paper snowflakes by using pipe cleaners.

> **Curriculum Suggestion:** Students can create a bar graph, data table, or other visual to illustrate different snowflakes that they collected or made. This is an easy way to integrate math and reading/interpreting data and charts.
>
> Science Process skills used are organizing, observing, classifying, collecting data, etc. A follow-up to this may be to "grow" crystals using borax or sugar in a classroom-controlled setting. See the following link for this activity (may be done together in class at grades K-1 and with supervision at Grade 2 and up): http://chemistry.about.com/cs/howtos/ht/boraxsnowflake.htm

> **Curriculum Suggestion:** In addition to paper cutout snowflakes, go outside (on a snowy/snowing day) and collect snowflakes on black construction paper; use a magnifying glass to observe the crystalline structures.

Materials
- Book: *The Snowy Day* by Ezra Jack Keats (Penguin Group, 1996)
- Real snow in a bowl (optional)
- Large mittens, boots, scarves, and hats
- Yarn balls or marshmallows
- White typing paper
- Wastebasket or a container to throw the snowballs in
- White paper footprints
- Mat
- 3 white-painted boxes of various sizes for snowman (they may be weighted with books or other materials to give them more stability)
- Snowman eyes, nose, mouth, and buttons cut out of construction paper
- Double-stick tape
- Cardboard window frame with plastic "glass" attached
- Cutout snowflakes
- Stencil and white paint or white bingo marker

Team: *Sari Micklewright, Lisa George, Nancy Morin, Beth Mosbach*

THEME: VEGETABLE GARDEN

LESSON PLAN (QUICK VIEW)

1. **Warm-Up:** Garden tools collection
2. **Vestibular:** Rabbit hopping in garden
3. **Proprioception:** Pretend body seeds
4. **Balance:** Balance beam vegetable picking
5. **Eye-Hand Coordination:** Vegetable toss
6. **Cool-Down:** Vegetable garden book
7. **Fine-Motor:** Dirt cake

1. WARM-UP
Place different gardening tools such as gloves, hand rake, hand shovel, pot, etc., at one end of the room and have the children take turns performing the wheelbarrow walk across the room to collect a tool. Explain what each tool is used for if the children are not familiar with them.

2. VESTIBULAR
Place a mat on the floor (cover with a brown sheet, brown paper, or brown polar fleece blanket to look like dirt). Have the children pretend to be rabbits and take turns hopping across the mat or floor, depending on the challenge level. The children could hop over the vegetables or gardening tools, hop forward, hop backward, and hop sideways with at least two turns for each child.

3. PROPRIOCEPTION
Tell the children they are going to pretend to be a seed that gets planted. Have each child roll up into a seed shape on the mat and place a beanbag chair on top of them. Lightly push down for mild compression. Have each child move into a tall kneeling position and stand up, pretending to grow up out of the ground.

4. BALANCE
Lay plastic or real vegetables on each side of a balance beam. Have the children walk forward, backward, and sideways on the balance beam, squatting to pick up a vegetable along the way. The children may place the vegetable in a basket at the end of the balance beam.

5. EYE-HAND COORDINATION
Using the vegetables from the balance activity, have the children toss the vegetables into a basket, one at a time, from a distance that is challenging but achievable for each child's ability level.

6. COOL-DOWN

Read a book about vegetable gardens. Discuss types of vegetables in a garden and take a survey to find out each child's favorite vegetable. Make a graph chart for the class totals. Discuss the importance of nutrition and exercise on health. Discuss the steps for planting a garden (dig a hole, plant a seed, water, and weed).
- *The Tale of Peter Rabbit* by Beatrix Potter (Warne, 2002)
- *Growing Vegetable Soup* by Lois Ehlert (Voyager Books, 1990)
- *From Seed to Plant* by Gail Gibbons (Holiday House, Inc., 1993)

> **Curriculum Suggestion:** One of the key concepts in the book *From Seed to Plant* is pollination of flowers in order to produce seeds and reproduce. This process is difficult for students to master. K-2 science standards state that students begin to develop an understanding of biological concepts. One such concept is the life cycles of plants.
>
> Instruct groups of children to become the key characters in the pollination process. Give students cards with names of the parts of the flower: pistil, stigma, anther and stamen, pollen grain, and petals. The children representing the anther flower parts should have some flour (to represent the pollen) dusted on their hands and arms. Label other cards with types of insects and birds: honeybees, butterflies, and hummingbirds. Ask the students to arrange themselves in a flower shape. They can refer to the pictures in the book. Next, tell the insects to move about the "flowers" and other insects. By doing this, the children will see that interactions between each player in the process is necessary in order for the pollen to be moved from flower to flower, thereby pollinating and causing seeds to grow.

7. FINE-MOTOR

Give each child two baggies, one with two Oreos™ and the other with 1/4 of a small package of chocolate pudding mix. Have the children crush their Oreos with a rolling pin or mallet or by using their hands. Have them add appropriate amounts of milk to the baggie with the pudding mix, re-close the bag, and shake and squish until the pudding thickens. Squeeze the pudding into a cup, sprinkle the top with crushed Oreos and top off with gummy worms. Enjoy!

> **Curriculum Suggestion:** If doing this activity with small groups, teach measuring volume to the nearest cup, pint, quart, or gallon. It is useful for students to experience comparing measurement amounts during a structured activity such as this. Generally, primary students should understand that cups are smaller than pints, quarts, or gallons but are larger than teaspoons, tablespoons, etc.

Materials
- Mat
- Brown sheet or blanket (optional)
- Beanbag chair
- Balance beam
- Plastic or real vegetables, different varieties
- Gardening tools such as gloves, hand shovel, hand rake, pot, etc.
- Basket or bucket
- Vegetable garden book (see suggestions under Cool-Down)
- Ziploc™ baggies
- Oreo cookies
- Chocolate pudding mix
- Gummy worms
- Milk
- Measuring cup
- Cups/bowls for pudding
- Spoons

Team: *Sandi Halron, Jean O'Flahrity, Sonja Bagley, Helen Kaiser, Jana Olson, Melissa Acker, Lisa Nikula*

THEME: WINTER

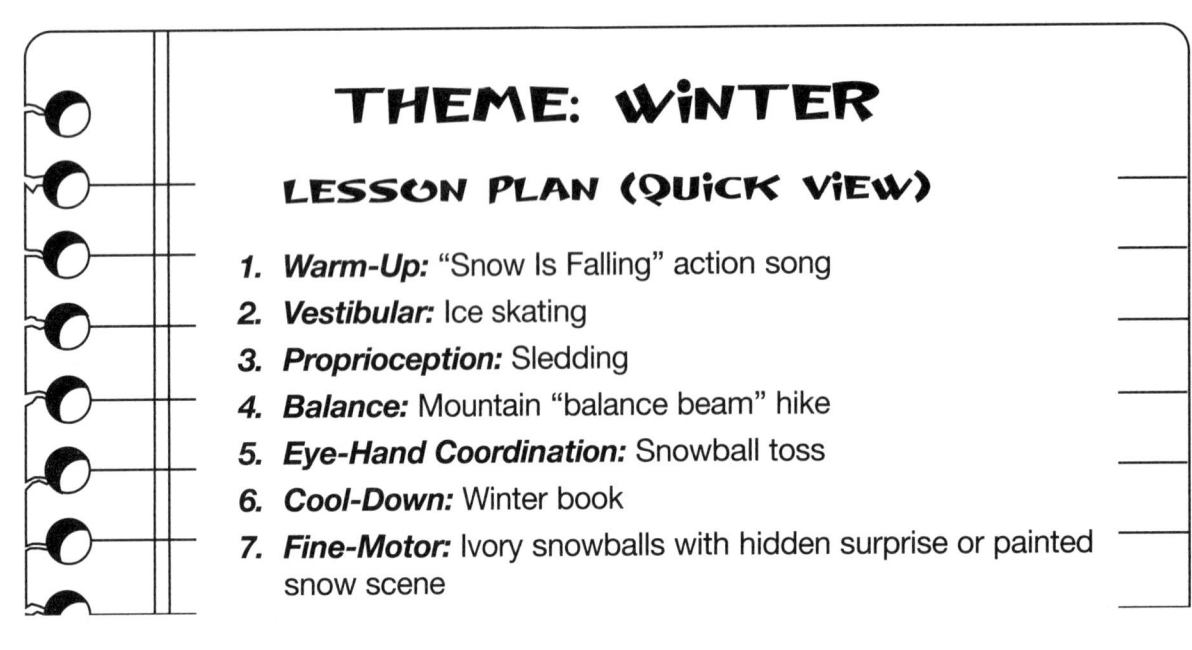

LESSON PLAN (QUICK VIEW)

1. **Warm-Up:** "Snow Is Falling" action song
2. **Vestibular:** Ice skating
3. **Proprioception:** Sledding
4. **Balance:** Mountain "balance beam" hike
5. **Eye-Hand Coordination:** Snowball toss
6. **Cool-Down:** Winter book
7. **Fine-Motor:** Ivory snowballs with hidden surprise or painted snow scene

1. WARM-UP

Have the children sing the following song and perform the associated actions while seated.
(Sung to: "Frère Jacques")

Snow is falling.
Snow is falling.
   (Raise arms into the air, while wiggling fingers; have the children slowly lower their arms to their sides)
In the air.
In the air.
   (Raise arms into the air and slowly swing arms back and forth to simulate snow falling)
Cold and white and fluffy.
Cold and white and fluffy.
   (Have the children give themselves a hug and pretend to shiver)
To the ground.
To the ground.
   (If seated, have the children lean over and touch the floor. If the children are standing, have them drop to the ground)

2. VESTIBULAR

Teach the children about snow and outdoor activities. Place a plastic shower curtain, paint tarp, or mat on the floor. Have the children remove their shoes and socks and practice skating across the floor by sliding their feet. Modalities may include shaving cream, paper plates, or styrofoam meat trays.

> **Curriculum Suggestion:** While the children are involved in this activity, it is a good time to practice letter, word, or numeral identification. Program the plastic tarp with any subject in the curriculum for the grade level. For younger

students, use pictures to represent phonics sounds or number sense. While the students are skating, they can announce the letter, number, sound, etc., that they land on. They can also be instructed to only skate on letters or numbers that spell words or write out their addresses/phone numbers, etc.

3. PROPRIOCEPTION

Tell the children to pretend that they are outdoors and will be sledding down a hill. To prepare for this activity, have scooter boards available for half the class. Match the children with a partner. As one student is sitting cross-legged on a scooter board holding on, the partner pushes her across the room. Once they have reached the opposite side of the room, have them rest and switch places.

If scooter boards are unavailable, prepare for this activity by filling a parachute (or sheet) with white balloons. Have the children hold on to the parachute and move it up and down to watch the "snow" balloons fall from the sky. The children can take turns going under the parachute (stuck in a snow drift) or sit inside the parachute (caught in a snow storm).

4. BALANCE

Create a snowdrift or a ridge of ice by placing a balance beam on the floor. Explain to the children that they will be going on a winter hike. Scatter paper snowflakes near the balance beam. Have the children take turns walking across the balance beam (forwards, backwards, sideways), picking up two matching snowflakes to drop into a winter cap placed at the far end of the balance beam.

5. EYE-HAND COORDINATION

Have the children crumple white paper into snowballs. Tell them to toss the snowballs into the snowman's hat or the length of a snowman's scarf. If the children miss the target, they are to gather all the snowballs into a pile and use a toy shovel to scoop them into the snowman's cap.

Curriculum Suggestion: Label the snowmen hats with vowels, numerals, letters of the alphabet, etc. Instruct students to aim for a certain snowman's hat when tossing the snowballs. They could accumulate points for getting it in the correct one. Tell older students to toss snowballs into three or more different-numbered hats. Label the hats "Addends." When they have tossed all their snowballs, the children collect them and report the "sum" to a team leader.

The same procedure may used with the letters of the alphabet, word families, contractions, parts of speech, punctuation marks, etc. The students could toss the snowballs into the appropriate hat to spell words, form contractions, identify nouns, verbs, or adjectives, or to color words.

Lesson Themes 143

6. COOL-DOWN

Read a book about winter. Have the children sit in a circle and wrap themselves in blankets. Discuss activities to do in the snow and how to dress appropriately when playing in the snow. Discuss how snow feels, what it looks like, where it comes from.

- *Snowballs* by Lois Ehlert (Harcourt Children's Books, 1999)
- *The Adventure of the Big Snow* by Nancy McArthur (Sagebrush Education Resources, 1998)
- *Snow Day* by Mercer Mayer (School Specialty Children's Publishing, 2001)

> **Curriculum Suggestion:** Demonstrating responsibility for their health is a benchmark for students in primary science classes. Another is observing weather and changes in the weather on a daily basis and discussing and understanding safety precautions for different kinds of weather. Create a graph of the number of days that have been safe enough for children to go sledding outdoors (if the activity is done in a climate that has snow). If there is not snow in your area, perhaps a class can become involved with an online collaborative project with a class in a different region. This will lead to many creative and thoughtful class discussions and data will become much more meaningful.

7. FINE-MOTOR

There are several options to choose from for a fine-motor activity, depending upon the age of the students.

A. Mix Ivory™ soap and water together to form a "snowball." Form the snowball around a small rubber ball so the children can "find" a toy surprise once they have used up the soap.

B. Create a snow scene by sponge painting or using cotton swabs to paint snow on blue construction paper. Another option is to glue cotton balls onto blue construction paper.

C. Mix shaving cream and glue together to create puffy paint. Use cotton swabs to make a snow scene on construction paper.

Materials

- Shower curtain or paint tarp
- Shaving cream
- Paper plates or clean styrofoam meat trays
- Scooter boards
- Balance beam
- Paper snowflakes to scatter on the floor
- Parachute, white balloons, or a white sheet
- Snowman hat or scarf
- Toy shovel
- Winter book (see suggestions under Cool-Down)
- Ivory™ soap

- Blue construction paper
- Small rubber ball
- Cotton balls, cotton swabs
- Shaving cream, glue
- Blankets

Team: *Nicole Giamos, Melissa Swedersky, Sally L. Hoftiezer*

THEME: ZOO

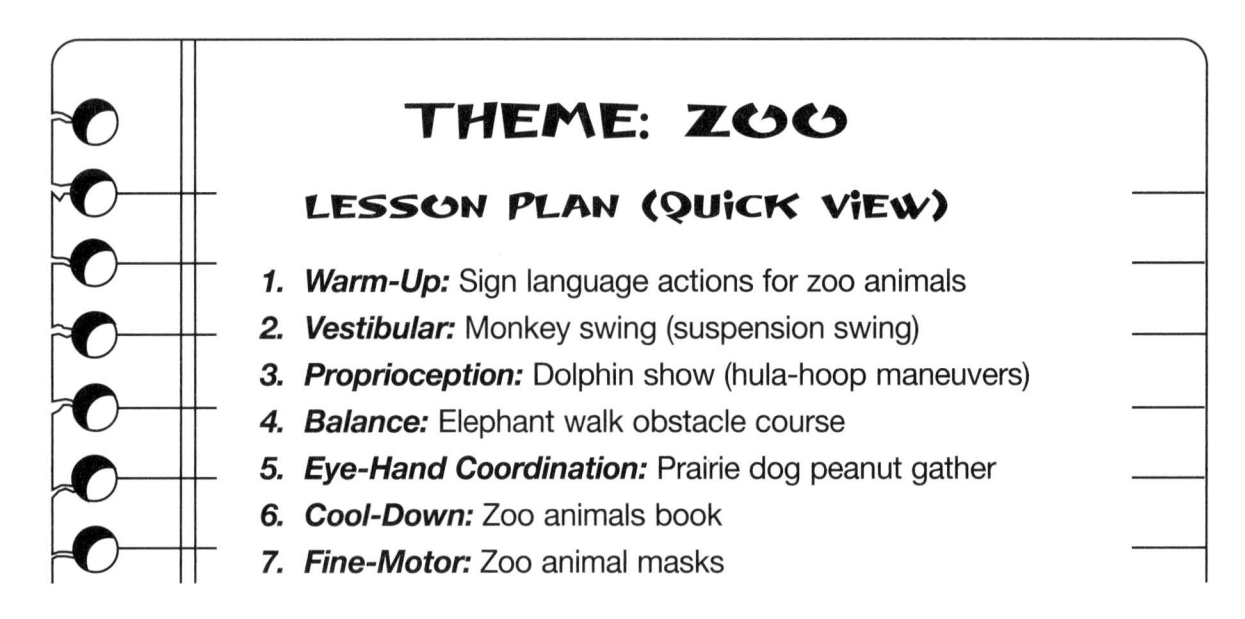

LESSON PLAN (QUICK VIEW)

1. **Warm-Up:** Sign language actions for zoo animals
2. **Vestibular:** Monkey swing (suspension swing)
3. **Proprioception:** Dolphin show (hula-hoop maneuvers)
4. **Balance:** Elephant walk obstacle course
5. **Eye-Hand Coordination:** Prairie dog peanut gather
6. **Cool-Down:** Zoo animals book
7. **Fine-Motor:** Zoo animal masks

1. WARM-UP

Teach sign language actions for each of the following animals: elephant, monkey, black bear, kangaroo, seal, lion, and bird. Have the children demonstrate actions. (See sign language action descriptions below.)

Elephant – Using a right curved "B" hand, trace an imaginary elephant's truck from nose outward.
Monkey – With curved hands, pantomime scratching sides as a monkey would.
Black bear – Cross arms over chest (left over right) with hands almost at opposite shoulders; make a scratching motion with all fingers.
Kangaroo – Hold curved "B" hands slightly in front of the body, palms down. Then move hands up and down twice to imitate the jumping of a kangaroo.
Seal – Place hands on side of the hip, facing the back of the body. Movement represents the movement of a seal's flippers.
Lion – Hold a cupped, open-fingered right hand at the hairline above forehead. Move the hand backward across the curve of the top of the head to illustrate the lion's mane.
Bird – Place the right "G" hand at the right side of mouth with fingers pointing forward, as if to create a bird's beak. Open and close the finger and thumb once or twice to emulate the movement of a bird's beak.

2. VESTIBULAR

Divide the children into two groups. One group will engage in Activity A while the other group engages in Activity B. After several turns, change groups so that each child gets a turn at both activities. Before beginning each activity, teach the children how our bodies move like animals in the environment and how our muscles work together to maintain us upright.

Activity A: While seated on a suspension swing or outdoor suspended platform rope, children take turns gently swinging each other reaching toward targets (8"x10" pictures of zoo animals).

Activity B: While balanced (pretzel sit/prone/or long seated) on scooter board, using a rope or thick cord (maximal 10 feet for young children), children maneuver themselves in the environment with reciprocal motions to pull toward targets.

> **Curriculum Suggestion:** Incorporate an estimation and data-gathering lesson into this activity. This will address a science and math benchmark for most primary classrooms. Prior to the children tugging themselves along the rope, show them how they can propel themselves quickly by pulling hard and then releasing the rope to see how far they will continue to "coast." After modeling, instruct students to make a prediction or estimate about how far they will roll. Record the predictions in a journal. (It works best on a smooth floor without a carpet, like a gymnasium floor.)
>
> Split the class into teams of 2-3. Each team member gets to attempt to "coast" three times. While one student does it, the other two can take turns measuring and recording the distances that the student coasts. Record results in a data tally chart. Once all team members have finished, teach the class how to convert their data from the table format to a bar graph. Rather than recording all three attempts by each team member, teach the students how to record the average of their trials.
>
> Conduct a class discussion to analyze the class's results. Be sure to ask the students to draw conclusions from the whole-class graph. For example, "Our class graph shows that you can go farther if you are smaller." "It doesn't matter if you are bigger and stronger. It's how fast you pull on the rope that matters."

3. PROPRIOCEPTION

Tell the children they are going to pretend to be dolphins. Use a hula-hoop in different ways to simulate dolphin "tricks." Hold the hula-hoop:
a. perpendicular to floor
b. placed on floor

Have the children (dolphins) go over/under/through the hula-hoop Spray a light mist over their heads to simulate under-water experience like dolphins at the zoo.

4. BALANCE

Have the children engage in elephant walking. Make feet patterns (described below) or obtain toy stilts (e.g., Romper Stompers, Playskool). Create a textured obstacle course with "gravel" (packing peanuts), "water" (blue tarp or sheet), or "boulders" (large rolled-up scrap paper), and/or create an obstacle course with classroom items such as chairs, re-arranged desks or tables, garbage cans, etc. Have the children take turns, intermittently spaced; walk with elephant feet (heavy stomping) with shoes on or off.

Elephant feet pattern: Using a black felt-tipped pen, make elephant toes on the grocery bags. Have children put bags on each foot. Tie tops with fabric scraps. Play music (*Lion King* sound track or *Jungle Book* elephant walk).

> **Curriculum Suggestion:** During this balance activity students can be fulfilling grade-level science and social studies benchmarks: Investigating properties of earth materials and the geographical landforms from which these earth materials originate.

5. EYE-HAND COORDINATION

Before the activity, draw a large tree shape on a 4-foot piece of large-roll construction paper. Tape on firm surface or wall. Choose two different colors and intermittently stencil twenty 2-inch circles on the "tree" (like apples on a poster tree). Next, attach 1-inch pieces of sticky-back Velcro on the inside of each circle. Attach the opposite side of Velcro to real or packing peanuts. Now stick Velcro peanuts to "tree."

Prepare two "prairie dogs" (coffee cans with picture of prairie dog attached to side and opening size 3-inch circle cut into top of coffee can lid).

To begin game, position two children in front of the "tree" and designate which color circle is theirs. Put a long brown tube sock on the students' arms (mother prairie dog). Place "prairie dog" (can) next to each of the two children, one for each to feed. Within 30 seconds, each child has to gather/pull as many "peanuts" as possible and feed them into the prairie dog can lid one at a time. Proceed by resetting the "peanuts" on the "tree" and having the next two children feed the "prairie dogs."

6. COOL-DOWN

Read a book about zoo animals such as one of those listed below. Discuss children's zoo trips, favorite animals, sounds each animal may make, foods the animals eat, etc.
- *Dear Zoo* by Rod Campbell (Simon & Schuster Children's, 2005)
- *Wild About Books* by Judy Sierra; illustrated by Marc Brown (Alfred A. Knopf Random House, 2004)
- *Animals in the Zoo* by Allen Fowler (Scholastic Library Publishing, 2000)

7. FINE-MOTOR

Make or purchase paper or foam masquerade masks or use paper plates – one for each child. Assemble decoration items, such as paper scraps, foam pieces (hole punch pieces make a great leopard, black fabric strips for tiger), feathers, etc. Children may use scissors or tear the scraps, and then use glue or paste to assemble their masks to work on fine-motor control. Another option involves using markers or paint to decorate masks. Have the children label their masks by tracing or copying their name on the back of the mask.

Materials

- Suspension swing
- 8"x10" zoo animal pictures and 2 prairie dog pictures
- Scooter board(s)
- 10-foot rope or thick cord (maximal length)
- Hula-hoop
- Spritz bottle filled with water
- Elephant feet grocery bags, rubber bands or ties made from an old sheet or toy stilts (Romper Stompers – Playskool)
- "Gravel" (packing peanuts), "water" (blue tarp or sheet), "boulders" (large rolled scrap paper)
- Music – *Lion King* sound track or *Jungle Book* recording for balance segment
- Construction roll paper
- Circle stencil
- 20 Velcro pieces
- 2 coffee cans with lids
- 4 brown tube socks
- Peanuts – real or packing
- Timer or clock
- Zoo animals book (see suggestions under Cool-Down)
- Masquerade masks – one for each child or 1/2 of paper plate for each child
- Paper scraps, foam pieces, black fabric strips feathers, paint, markers (mask decorations)
- Paste, scissors, hole punch, markers

Team: *Lori Curtis, Shelley Hertz, Mary McIntire-Belter*

REFERENCES

Ahn, R. R., Miller, L. J., Milberger, S., & McIntosh, D. N. (2004). Prevalence of parents' perceptions of sensory processing disorders among kindergarten children. *American Journal of Occupational Therapy, 58,* 287-293.

Allgood, N. (2005). *Music therapy: The use of music to address sensory issues.* Dallas, TX: S.I. Focus Magazine.

Ayres, A. J. (1979). *Sensory integration and the child.* Los Angeles: Western Psychological Services.

Baptiste, B. (2004). *My daddy is a pretzel.* Cambridge, MA: Barefoot Books.

Baranek, G. (2002). Efficacy of sensory and motor interventions for children with autism. *Journal of Autism and Developmental Disorders, 32*(5), 397-442.

Barol, J. (2007). *The effects of animal-assisted therapy on a child with autism.* Unpublished study. New Mexico Highland University School of Social Work, Albuquerque, NM.

Batsch, G., Elliott, J., Graden, J., Grimes, J., Kovaleski, J., Prasse, D. et al. (2006). *Response to intervention: Policy considerations and implementation.* Alexandria, VA: NASDSE

Behar, M. (2005, June 13). Using yoga to treat autism. *Advance for Occupational Therapy Practitioners, 21*(12), 27.

Brack, J. C. (2004). *Learn to move, move to learn sensorimotor early childhood activity themes.* Shawnee Mission, KS: Autism Asperger Publishing Company.

Brunhoff, L. (2002). *Babar's yoga for elephants.* New York: Harry N. Abrams, Inc.

Bundy, A., Lane, S., & Murray, E. (2002). *Sensory integration theory and practice* (2nd ed.). Philadelphia: F. A. Davis Company.

Davies, P. L., & Gavin, W. J. (2007). Validating the diagnosis of sensory processing disorders using EEG technology. *American Journal of Occupational Therapy, 61,* 176-189.

Dunn, W. (1999). *Sensory profile.* San Antonio, TX: The Psychological Corporation. A Harcourt Assessment Company.

Dunn, W. (2002). *Infant toddler sensory profile user's manual.* San Antonio, TX: The Psychological Corporation A Harcourt Assessment Company.

Dunn, W. (2006). *Sensory profile school companion.* San Antonio, TX: The Psychological Corporation A Harcourt Assessment Company.

Fertel-Daly, D., Bedell, G., & Hinojosa, J. (2001). Effects of a weighted vest on attention to task and self-stimulatory behaviors in preschoolers with pervasive developmental disorders. *American Journal of Occupational Therapy, 55,* 629-640.

Gioia, G., Isquith, P., Guy, S., & Kenworthy, L. (1996). *Behavior rating inventory of executive function.* Lutz, FL: Psychological Assessment Resources.

Hall, L., & Case-Smith, J. (2007). The effect of sound-based intervention on children with sensory processing disorders and visual-motor delays. *American Journal of Occupational Therapy, 61,* 209-215.

Heiberger, D. W., & Heiniger-White, M. C. (2000). *S'cool moves for learning.* Shasta, CA: Integrated Learner Press.

Hendon, C., & Bohon, L. M. (2008). Hospitalized children's mood differences during play and music therapy. *Child: Care, Health, and Development, 34*(2), 141-144.

Henry, D., Kane-Wineland, M., & Swindeman, S. (2007). *Tools for tots: Sensory strategies for toddlers and preschoolers.* Glendale, AZ: Henry Occupational Therapy Services, Inc.

Henry, D., & Sava, D. (2006). *Sensory tools for pets: Animals and people helping each other.* Glendale, AZ: Henry Occupational Therapy Services, Inc.

Henry, D. (2001). *Tool chest: For teachers, parents and students.* Glendale, AZ: Henry Occupational Therapy Services, Inc.

Honaker, D., & Rossi, L. M. (2005). Proprioception and participation at school: Are weighted vests effective? Appraising the evidence parts 1 and 2. *Sensory Integration Special Interest Section Quarterly, 3 & 4.*

Jarrett, O. S., & Maxwell, D. M. (2000). *What research says about the need for recess. In Elementary school recess: Selected readings, games, and activities for teachers and parents* (pp. 12-23). Lake Charles, LA: American Press.

Jarrett, O. S., Maxwell, D. M., Dickerson, C., Hoge, P., Davies, G., & Yetley, A. (1998). The impact of recess on classroom behavior: Group effects and individual differences. *Journal of Educational Research, 92*(2), 121-126.

Jensen, E. (1998). *Teaching with the brain in mind.* Alexandria, VA: Association for Supervision and Curriculum Development.

Kraft, R. E. (1989). Children at play: Behavior of children at recess. *Journal of Physical Education, Recreation, and Dance, 53*(3), 55-58.

May-Benson, T. (2007). *Goal attainment scaling manual.* Presentation at the American Occupational Therapy annual conference, St. Louis, MO.

Miller, L. J., & Fuller, D. A. (2006). Sensational kids: *Hope and help for children with sensory processing disorder.* New York: G. P. Putnam's Sons, a member of Penguin Group, Inc.

Miller, L. J., Anzalone M. E., Lane, S. J., Cermak, S. A., & Osten, E. T. (2007). Concept evolution in sensory integration: A proposed nosology for diagnosis. *American Journal of Occupational Therapy, 61,* 135-140.

Parham, L. D., Ecker, C., Miller Kuhaneck, H., Henry, D. A., & Glennon, T. J. (2007) *Sensory Processing Measure (SPM): Manual.* Los Angeles: Western Psychological Services.

Pellegrini, A. D. (1995). *School recess and playground behavior.* Albany: State University of New York.

Pellegrini, A. D., & Davis, P. L. (1993) Relations between children's playground and classroom behaviour. *British Journal of Educational Psychology, 63*(1), 88-95.

Peterson, D. A., & Thaut, M. H. (2007). Music increases frontal EEG coherence during verbal learning. *Neuroscience Letters, 412*(3), 217-221.

Pfeiffer, B., Henry, A., Miller, S., & Witherell, S. (2008). Effectiveness of disc 'o' sit cushions on attention to task in second-grade students with attention difficulties. American *Journal of Occupational Therapy, 62,* 274-281.

Puliti, B. (2007, January 8). Standing room only. *Advance for Occupational Therapy Practitioners, 23*(1), 40-41.

Ramachandran, V., & Oberman, L. (2006). Broken mirrors: A theory of autism. *Scientific American, 295*(5), 63-69.

Rauscher, F. H., Shaw, G. L., & Ky, K. N. (1995). Listening to Mozart enhances spatial-temporal reasoning: towards a neurophysiological basis. *Neuroscience Letters, 185*(1), 44-47.

Rimland, B. (1990). Sound sensitivity in autism. *Autism Research Review International, 4*(1), 6.

Rizzolatti, G., Fogassi, L., & Gallese, V. (2006). Mirrors in the mind. *Scientific American, 295*(5), 54-61.

Rosenblum, S., Goldstand, S., & Parush, S. (2006). Relationships among biomechanical ergonomic factors, handwriting product quality, handwriting efficiency, and computerized handwriting process measures in children with and without handwriting difficulties. *American Journal of Occupational Therapy, 60*, 28-39.

Sams, M. J., Fortney, E. V., & Willenbring, S. (2006). Occupational therapy incorporating animals for children with autism: A pilot investigation. *American Journal of Occupational Therapy, 60*, 268-274.

Schilling, D., & Schwartz, I. (2004). Alternative seating for young children with autism spectrum disorder: Effects on classroom behavior. *Journal of Autism and Developmental Disorders, 34*, 423-432.

Schilling, D., Washington, K., Billingsley, F., & Deitz, J. (2003). Classroom seating for children with attention deficit hyperactivity disorder: Therapy balls versus chairs. *American Journal of Occupational Therapy, 57*, 534-541.

Tomchek, S., & Dunn, W. (2007). Sensory processing in children with and without autism: A comparative study using the short sensory profile. *American Journal of Occupational Therapy, 61*, 190-200.

VandenBerg, N. (2001). The use of a weighted vest to increase on-task behavior in children with attention difficulties. *American Journal of Occupational Therapy, 55*, 621-628.

Wallis, C. (May 15, 2006). Inside the autistic mind. *Time Magazine.* www.time.com/time/

Wilbarger, P., & Wilbarger, J. L. (1991). *Sensory defensiveness in children aged 2-12. An intervention guide for parents and other caretakers.* Denver, CO: Avanti Educational Programs.

Wilkinson, L., Scholey, A., & Wesnes, K. (2002). Chewing gum selectively improves aspects of memory in healthy volunteers. *Appetite, 38*, 235-236.

Williams, D. L., Goldstein, G., & Minshew, N. J. (2006). The profile of memory function in children with autism. *Neuropsychology, 20*, 21-29.

Williams, M. S., & Shellenberger, S. (1996). *How does your engine run? A Leader's guide to the alert program for self-regulation.* Albuquerque, NM: Therapy Works, Inc.

Williamson, G., & Anzalone, M. (2001). *Sensory integration and self-regulation in infants and toddlers: Helping very young children interact with their environments.* Washington, DC: Zero to Three.

APPENDIX

Teacher Observation Checklist

Student Name:_____ **Date:**_____
Date of Birth:_____**School/Grade:**_____
Teacher:_____**Planning Period:**_____
Best time of day to observe problem:_____
Return to occupational therapist by:_____

Please check appropriate boxes.

Sensory Organization
- ☐ Runs into desks, doors, or people
- ☐ Does not know body parts (elbow, wrist, etc.)
- ☐ Has poor tolerance for touch
- ☐ Has poor tolerance for hands in paste, finger paint, or messy materials
- ☐ Does not identify right and left on self and papers
- ☐ Has not established hand preference
- ☐ Cannot cross midline of body with either hand
- ☐ Does not know directional concepts
- ☐ Moves excessively in chair
- ☐ Slumps at desk/leans on desk

Behavior
- ☐ Demonstrates inadequate attention span for age
- ☐ Demonstrates inconsistent performance level
- ☐ Demonstrates aggressive actions toward others
- ☐ Demonstrates impulsiveness
- ☐ Easily distracted by auditory or visual stimuli

Fine-Motor Skills
- ☐ Holds pencil or crayon incorrectly
- ☐ Holds scissors incorrectly
- ☐ Controls pencil with difficulty
- ☐ Controls scissors with difficulty
- ☐ Fatigues during fine-motor tasks
- ☐ Has difficulty stabilizing paper when writing
- ☐ Has difficulty manipulating paper when cutting
- ☐ Writes too slowly or too fast (circle one)

From Brack, J. C. (2009). *Learn to Move, Moving Up!* Shawnee Mission, KS: Autism Asperger Publishing Company. Used with permission.

Visual Motor/Perceptual
☐ Does not recognize shapes and letters
☐ Cannot copy   O circle   + plus   ☐ square   △ triangle (please circle)
☐ Forms letters incorrectly
☐ Does not keep letters on baseline when writing
☐ Maintains poor spacing between words/letters
☐ Makes letter reversals (typical through 1st grade)
☐ Changes paper orientation when writing
☐ Has difficulty copying from far point
☐ Cannot organize work/desk
☐ Colors outside of boundary lines
☐ Does not stay on the line when cutting
☐ Cannot assemble age-appropriate puzzles independently
☐ Loses place on page when reading
☐ Holds book too close or too far away (circle one)
☐ Wears glasses

Functional Skills
☐ Unable to button, zip, snap, or tie shoes (circle all that apply)
☐ Needs adaptive equipment to function in classroom (list equipment)
☐ Has difficulty finding way to familiar places at school (cafeteria, office, bathroom)
☐ Does not follow directions or remember routines
☐ Demonstrates poor self help skills: eating, dressing, hand washing, other_____ (circle)

Attach handwriting samples if area of concern.

Comments/Concerns:_____

_____
_____
_____
_____
_____
_____
_____
_____

From Brack, J. C. (2009). *Learn to Move, Moving Up!* Shawnee Mission, KS: Autism Asperger Publishing Company. Used with permission.

Adapted School Supply List

I have found the following school supplies, adapted from a traditional school supply list, to be particularly helpful for students; however, many other products are also beneficial and there are many other opinions concerning preferred products. Consult an occupational therapist to identify items that specifically match an individual student's needs.

- ☐ **Crayola® Pip-Squeaks™ markers**
  These short markers are easier to grasp than regular-length markers.
  Purchase from most discount stores.

- ☐ **Crayola® Mini Twistable crayons**
  These short crayons are easier to grasp than regular-length crayons; besides, they work well for students who color with heavy pressure as they do not break because they are encased in a plastic shell.
  Purchase from most discount stores.

- ☐ **FLIP Crayons™**
  These are recommended as a classroom purchase because they come in a box of 206 or 20 mini-packs of 5. The short size is easier for students to grasp and two colors on one crayon helps hands develop coordination for improved coloring/writing skills.
  Purchase from www.HWTears.com.

- ☐ **Pencils for Little Hands**
  These are recommended as a classroom purchase because they come in a box of 144. The short length is easier to grasp than a regular-length pencil. For kindergarten, first- and second-grade students.
  Purchase from www.HWTears.com.

- ☐ **Mechanical Pencil**
  A mechanical pencil helps students who frequently break their pencil lead from writing with heavy pencil pressure, because it allows students to have a sharpened pencil lead instantly. For third-, fourth-, fifth-, and sixth-grade students.
  Purchase from most discount stores.

- ☐ **Puffs® Plus facial tissue (with lotion)**
  These facial tissues are softer than other brands and help to minimize sensory-sensitive noses.
  Purchase from any grocery store or pharmacy.

- ☐ **Bright Lines® handwriting paper**
  This type of handwriting paper provides a visual cue for letter placement with a yellow highlight.
  Purchase from www.brightlinespaper.com.

- ☐ **Handwriting Without Tears® Draw & Write/Writing Notebook**
  This handwriting notebook paper can be used with schools or individual students who utilize the Handwriting Without Tears® handwriting program.
  Purchase from www.HWTears.com.

- ☐ **Spaceman handwriting spacers**
  These are recommended as a classroom purchase because they come in a set of 30. The painted clothespin spacers are motivating for students to use for spacing accurately between words when writing.
  Purchase from www.reallygoodstuff.com.

From Brack, J. C. (2009). *Learn to Move, Moving Up!* Shawnee Mission, KS: Autism Asperger Publishing Company. Used with permission.

- ☐ **The Writing C.L.A.W. pencil grip**
  This pencil grip allows students to place fingers accurately on the pencil with little effort and maintains a functional grasp pattern for writing.
  Purchase from www.writingclaw.com.

- ☐ **Fiskar® scissors**
  These scissors work for both right- and left-handed students. The design is user friendly, allowing the scissors to cut even if slightly tilted.
  Purchase from most discount stores.

- ☐ **Crayola® No-Drip Gel paint**
  These paints are recommended in place of watercolor paints because they have a thick consistency and thus stick to a paintbrush more readily than water color paints; they also easily adhere to paper.
  Purchase from most discount stores.

- ☐ **PackSmart™ backpack**
  This backpack is ergonomically beneficial. It helps to minimize strain on the back because it is made of light-weight material, has padded shoulder straps and a low back pad to distribute the weight evenly, and is a child-sized fit.
  Purchase from www.Integrationscatalog.com.

- ☐ **ChewEase Pencil Topper™**
  This product is helpful for students who have the need to chew for calming or concentration. It is made of clear flexible plastic, has a tubular shape to fit over the tip of a standard pencil, and is useful when gum chewing is not allowed.
  Purchase from www.Integrationscatalog.com.

- ☐ **Pencil fidgets**
  These are helpful for students who need to keep their hands busy in order to pay attention. The fidgets easily fit on the end of a pencil, making them readily available for students to use in a school setting. They come in four different designs (Spin Snapper, Nut N' Bolt, Wingnut, and Bump N' Run Maze).
  Purchase from www.Abilitations.com.

- ☐ **Seat Sack™ organizer**
  These are recommended as a classroom purchase to use on every student's chair for organizing homework papers, books, notes home, etc. They can be re-used from year to year.
  Purchase from www.seatsack.com.

Commonly Available School Supplies

- ☐ Elmer's washable glue
- ☐ Glue stick – purple or blue
- ☐ Plastic school box organizer
- ☐ Zipper bag for pencils
- ☐ Pocket folders
- ☐ Rubber eraser

May be purchased from most discount stores.

From Brack, J. C. (2009). *Learn to Move, Moving Up!* Shawnee Mission, KS: Autism Asperger Publishing Company. Used with permission.

Definitions

Amygdala: Part of the limbic system that plays a role in processing emotions and memory, and contributes to social behavior.

Ayres Sensory Integration® (ASI): Developed by A. Jean Ayres; is the basis for intervention that uses sensory input for meaningful, active participation and interaction.

Cerebellum: Located at the base of the skull in the posterior part of the brain. Functions for smooth, coordinated motor movements, newly learned motor skills; also regulates muscle tone.

Corpus callosum: A massive bundle of nerve fibers that separate the right and left cerebral hemispheres of the brain.

Frontal lobe: The largest and most anterior part of the brain responsible for planning, problem solving, and executing behavior.

Hippocampus: Forms part of the limbic system in the brain and functions for memory, motivation, and attention.

Limbic system: A group of interconnected brain structures that function for olfaction, emotion, motivation, and behavior.

Neurotransmitter: Chemical substance, such as serotonin, norepinephrine, and epinephrine, that transmits nerve impulses across a gap.

Nosology: The systematic classification of diseases for medical science.

Mirror neurons: Recently discovered nerve cells located in the brain that act as a mirror mechanism, allowing the observer to imitate others' actions.

Proprioceptive system: Made up of receptors in the joints, muscles, and tendons; provides awareness of body position in space.

Sensory diet: Sensory strategies that are incorporated into daily routines and spaced apart for specific lengths of time to help an individual attain a "just right" (Williams & Shellenberger, 1996, pp. 2-3) alertness state (e.g., carrying heavy books, running office errand, chewing on a straw).

Sensory strategies: Simple solutions that can be easily implemented in a variety of environments and circumstances to address sensory needs.

Vestibular system: Made up of receptors in the inner ear and stimulated by movement for direction, speed, and orientation.

White matter: The part of the brain that is composed of nerve fibers, which are insulated by a whitish, fatty sheath (myelin).

PRODUCTS & RESOURCES

Abilitations
P.O. Box 922668
Norcross, GA 30010-2668
1-800-850-8602
www.abilitations.com

Harcourt Assessment, Inc.
19500 Bulverde Road
San Antonio, TX 78259
1-800-211-8378
www.harcourtassessment.com

Henry OT Services, Inc.
7942 W. Bell Road #C5-429
Glendale, AZ 85389
E-Mail: rick@henryot.com
1-623-882-8812
www.ateachabout.com

Integrations
P.O. Box 922668
Norcross, GA 30010-2668
1-800-850-8602
www.integrationscatalog.com

OT Vest™, LLC
4646 Wishing Well Ct.
Portage, MI 49024
1-269-329-3287
www.Otvest.com

Pearson/AGS
5601 Green Valley Drive
Bloomington, MN 55437-1187
1-800-627-7271
ags.pearsonassessments.com

Ready Bodies, Learning Minds
20475 Highway 46 West
Suite 180-144
Spring Branch, TX 78070
1-866-865-3781
www.readybodies.com

Route 2 Greatness
P.O. Box 116
Ingomar, PA 15127-011
1-412-498-6555
www.route2greatness.com

S'cool Moves®
P.O.Box 614
Shasta, CA 96087
1-866-232-5446
www.schoolmoves.com

Southpaw Enterprises, Inc.
800 West Third St.
Dayton, OH 45407-2805
1-800-228-1698
www.southpawenterprises.com

Speed Stacks, Inc.
14 Inverness Drive, D-100
Englewood, CO 80112
1-877-GOT-CUPS (877-468-2877)
www.speedstacks.com

Therapro
225 Arlington St.
Framingham, MA 01702-8723
1-800-257-5376
www.theraproducts.com

Vital Links
6613 Seybold Road, Suite E
Madison, WI 53719
Phone: (608) 270-5424
Continuing Education for Therapeutic Listening®
www.vitallinks.net

Websites

www.alertprogram.com
How Does Your Engine Run? Program teaching children sensory self-regulation

www.aota.org
American Occupational Therapy Association, Inc. website

www.autismawarenesscentre.org
Canada-based autism resources website

www.gymnic.com
Manufactures and distributes Disc 'O Sit cushions

www.jimcosgrove.com
Children's singer and songwriter

www.kidsexpresstrain.com
Educational children's songs with activities

www.nasdse.org
National Association of State Directors of Special Education, Inc. Response to Intervention project information

www.out-of-sync-child.com
Carol Kranowitz's website with information about sensory processing disorder

www.pubmedcentral.com
Research website

www.researchtopractice.info
Research website

www.skipwest.com
Music for children, families, and educators

www.SongsForTeaching.com
Theme-based children's songs for download purchase

www.spdconnection.com
Jenny Clark Brack's website with information about sensory processing disorder

www.spdfoundation.net
This site includes sensory processing disorder information for parents, teachers, and therapists

www.siglobalnetwork.org
International website providing information on Ayres Sensory Integration® (ASI)

www.spioworks.com
Makes and sells Stabilizing Pressure Input Orthosis

www.underarmour.com
Manufactures and distributes breathable pressure garments

RECOMMENDED CHILDREN'S BOOKS

(Arranged by Lesson Theme)

Baseball
- *The BL Counting Book* by Barbara Barbieri McGrath; illustrated by Brian Shaw (Charlesbridge Publishing, Inc., 1999)
- *The Berenstain Bears Play Ball* by Stan and Jan Berenstain (HarperCollins Publishers, 2004)

Birthday Party
- *If You Give a Pig a Party* by Laura Numeroff (HarperCollins Publishers, 2005)
- *The Mouse, the Cat, and Grandmother's Hat* by Nancy Willard (Little, Brown & Company, 2003)
- *I Like Birthdays ... It's the Parties I'm Not Sure About* by Laurie Renke; illustrated by Jake and Max Renke (Sensory Resources, 2005)

Bugs
- *The Very Busy Spider* by Eric Carle (Penguin Young Readers Group, 1989)
- *The Very Quiet Cricket* by Eric Carle (Penguin Young Readers Group, 1997)
- *Bug Dance* by Stuart J. Murphy (HarperCollins Publishers, 2001)

Camping
- *Curious George Goes Camping* by Margret & H. A. Rey (Houghton Mifflin Company, 1999)
- *Fred and Ted Go Camping* by Peter Eastman (Random House Children's Books, 2005)
- *Bailey Goes Camping* by Kevin Henkes (HarperCollins Publishers, 1985)
- *Amelia Bedelia Goes Camping* by Peggy Parish (Greenwillow Books, 1985)

Car Wash
- *The Scrubbly-Bubbly Car Wash* by Irene O'Garden (HarperCollins Publishers, 2003)
- *Five Little Monkeys Wash the Car* by Eileen Christelow (Houghton Mifflin Company, 2004)
- *Sluggers' Car Wash* by Stuart J. Murphy and Barney Slatzberg (HarperCollins Publishers, 2002)

Caterpillars
- *Caterpillars* by Karen Stray Nolting (Houghton Mifflin Company, 2000)
- *From Caterpillar to Butterfly* by Deborah Heiligman; illustrated by Bari Weissman (HarperCollins Publishers, 1996)

Clouds
- *Little Cloud* by Eric Carle (Penguin Young Readers Group, 1998)
- *Crazy About Clouds* by Rena Korb and Brandon Reibeling (Looking Glass Library, 2007)
- *What Do You See in a Cloud?* by Allan Fowler (Sagebrush Education Resources, 1996)

Down on the Farm
- *Down on the Farm* by Merrily Kutner & Will Killenbrand (Holiday House, Inc., 2005)
- *Over on the Farm* by Christopher Gunson (Random House UK, 2003)
- *Farm Life* by Elizabeth Spurr (Holiday House Inc., 2003)
- *The Day Jimmy's Boa Ate the Wash* by Trinka Hakes (Penguin Young Readers Group, 1992)

Fall Fun
- *Trick or Treat Little Critter* by Gina Mayer and Mercer Mayer (Random House Children's Books, 1993)
- *Apples and Pumpkins* by Anne Rockwell (Simon & Schuster Children's Publishing, 2005)
- *Picking Apples and Pumpkins* by Amy Hutchings (Scholastic Inc., 1994)

Fiesta or Cinco De Mayo
- *Fiesta!* by June Behrens (Scholastic Library Publishing, 1986)
- *Cinco De Mayo* by Ann Heinrichs; illustrated by Kathleen Petelinsek (The Child's World Inc., 2006)

Finding Escaped Zoo Animals (Equestrian Therapy)
- *Hippotherapy – A Trudie Small Book Series on Children's Health Matters* by Deborah A. Tayler (Deborah A. Tayler, 2004)

Flower Garden
- *City Green* by DyAnne DiSalvo-Ryan (HarperCollins Publishers, 1994)
- *Sunflower House* by Eve Bunting (Voyager Books, 1999)

Football/Green Bay Packers
- *If I Were a Green Bay Packer* by Joseph C. D'Andrea (Picture Me Books, 1994).
- *Football* by Salina Yoon (Simon & Schuster Children's Publishing, 2005)
- *Football Friends* by Jean Marzollo, Dan Marzollo, Dave Marzollo (Sagebrush Education Resources, 1997)
- *Kick the Football, Charlie Brown!* by Charles M. Schultz, adapted by Judy Katschke (Simon & Schuster Children's Publishing, 2001)
- *Kick, Pass, And Run* by Leonard Kessler (HarperCollins Children's Books, 1996)

Fourth of July
- *Hooray for the Fourth of July* by Rick Brown (Sterling Publishing, 2007)
- *The Fourth of July Story* by Alice Dalgliesh (Simon & Schuster Children's Publishing, 1995)
- *Red, White and Blue: The Story of the American Flag* by John Herman (Penguin Young Readers Group, 1998)

Garden
- *How Groundhog's Garden Grew* by Lynne Cherry (Blue Sky Press, 2003)
- *And the Good Brown Earth* by Kathy Henderson (Candlewick Press, 2003)

Halloween
- *It's the Great Pumpkin, Charlie Brown* by Charles M. Schulz (Perseus Publishing, 2004)
- *The Hallo-Wiener* by Dav Pilkey (The Blue Sky Press, 1995)
- *Inside a House That Is Haunted* by Alyssa Satin Capucilli; illustrated by Tedd Arnold (Scholastic Inc. Cartwheel Books, 1998)

Insects
- *Charlie the Caterpillar* by Dom DeLuise (Simon & Schuster Children's Publishing, 1993)
- *How to Hide a Butterfly & Other Insects* by Ruth Heller (Penguin Young Readers Group, 1992)

Laundry
- *Fox in Socks* by Dr. Seuss. (Random House, Inc., 1965)
- *Caillou The Missing Sock* by Sarah Margaret Johnson (Chouette Publishing, 2003)
- *Froggy Gets Dressed* by Jonathan London; illustrated by Frank Remkiewicz (Penguin Books, 1992)

Mardi Gras/100th School Day
- *Mimi's First Mardi Gras* by Alice W. Couvillon; illustrated by Elizabeth Moore (Pelican Publishing Company, Inc., 1992)
- *On Mardi Gras Day* by Fatima Shaik (Dial Books for Young Readers, 1999)
- *The Night Before the 100th Day of School* by Natasha Wing; illustrated by Mindy Pierce (Penguin Young Readers Group, 2005)
- *100th Day Worries* by Margery Cuyler; illustrated by Arthur Howard (Simon & Schuster Children's Publishing, 2005)

Outer Space
- *Looking at the Planets: A Book About the Solar System* by Melvin Berger (Tandem Library Books, 1995)
- *Planet Earth/Inside Out* by Gail Gibbons (HarperCollins Publishers, 1998)

Pigs
- *Mrs. Piggle Wiggle's Farm* by Betty MacDonald (HarperCollins Publishers, 1985)
- *Pigsty* by Mark Teague (Scholastic, 1994)

Police
- *I'm Going to Be a Police Officer* by Edith Kunhardt (Scholastic, 1995)
- *A Day at the Police Station* by Richard Scarry (Golden Books, 2004)

Puppies
- *Just Me and My Puppy* by Mercer Mayer (Golden Books, 1998)
- *Poor Puppy* by Nick Bruel (Roaring Brook Press, 2007)

Snow
- *The Snowflake: A Water Cycle Story* by Neil Waldman (Lerner Publishing Group, 2003)
- *Snowflake Bentley* by Jacqueline Briggs Martin (Houghton Mifflin Company, 1998)
- *Millions of Snowflakes* by Mary McKenna Siddals (Houghton Mifflin Company, 1998)

Snowman
- *The Biggest, Best Snowman* by Margery Cuyler (Scholastic, 2004)
- *All You Need for a Snowman* by Alice Schertle (Harcourt, 2007)
- *Snowmen at Night* by Caralyn Buehner (Dial, 2003)
- *Snowmen at Christmas* by Caralyn Buehner (Dial Books for Young Readers, 2005)
- *Snowman in a Box* by Nancy Armstrong (Perseus Publishing, 2004)

Spring Flowers
- *When the Wind Stops* by Charlotte Zolotow (HarperCollins Children's Books, 1997)
- *Grandma's Purple Flowers* by Adjoa J. Burrowes (Lee & Low Books, Inc., 2000)

The Snowy Day
- *The Snowy Day* by Ezra Jack Keats (Penguin Group, 1996)

Vegetable Garden
- *The Tale of Peter Rabbit* by Beatrix Potter (Warne, 2002)
- *Growing Vegetable Soup* by Lois Ehlert (Voyager Books, 1990)
- *From Seed to Plant* by Gail Gibbons (Holiday House, Inc., 1993)

Winter
- *Snowballs* by Lois Ehlert (Harcourt Children's Books, 1999)
- *The Adventure of the Big Snow* by Nancy McArthur (Sagebrush Education Resources, 1998)
- *Snow Day* by Mercer Mayer (School Specialty Children's Publishing, 2001)

Zoo
- *Dear Zoo* by Rod Campbell (Simon & Schuster Children's, 2005)
- *Wild About Books* by Judy Sierra; illustrated by Marc Brown (Alfred A. Knopf-Random House, 2004)
- *Animals in the Zoo* by Allen Fowler (Scholastic Library Publishing, 2000)

APC

Autism Asperger Publishing Co.
P.O. Box 23173
Shawnee Mission, Kansas 66283-0173
www.asperger.net